EDGAR CAYCE ON ATLANTIS

by Edgar Evans Cayce

under the editorship of

Hugh Lynn Cayce

Director, Association for Research and Enlightenment

WARNER BOOKS

A Warner Communications Company

GN
751
.C35
PHP
C.2

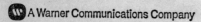
2578

TO

My Wife and Children

whose patience and cooperation helped a great deal

in the preparation of this book

CONTENTS

PREFACE

Who was Edgar Cayce?

The six books which have been written about him have totaled more than a million in sales, and more than ten other books have devoted sections to his life and talents. He has been featured in dozens of magazines and hundreds of newspaper articles dating from 1900 to the present. What was so unique about him?

It depends upon your point of view. A number of his contemporaries knew the "waking" Edgar Cayce as a gifted professional photographer. Another group (predominantly children) admired him as a warm and friendly Sunday School teacher. His own family knew him as a wonderful husband and father.

The "sleeping" Edgar Cayce was an entirely different figure, a psychic known to thousands of people in all walks of life. Many had cause to be grateful for his help; indeed, some of them believe that he alone either saved or changed their lives when all seemed lost. The "sleeping" Edgar Cayce was a medical diagnostician, a prophet, and a devoted proponent of Bible lore.

In June 1954, the University of Chicago held him in sufficient esteem to accept a Ph.D. thesis based on a study of his life and work: in this thesis the author referred to him as a "religious seer." That same June, the children's comic book *House of Mystery* bestowed on him the impressive title of "America's Most Mysterious Man!"

Even as a child on a farm near Hopkinsville, Kentucky, where he was born on March 18, 1877, Edgar Cayce displayed powers of perception which seemed to extend beyond the normal range of the five senses. At the age of six or seven he told his parents that he was able to see and talk to "visions," sometimes of relatives who had recently died. His parents attributed this to the overactive imagination of a lonely child who had been influenced by the dramatic language of the revival meetings which were popular in that section of the country. Later, by sleeping with his head on his schoolbooks, he developed a form of photographic memory which helped him advance rapidly in the country school. This faded, however, and Edgar was only able to complete the seventh grade before he had to seek his own place in the world.

In 1898 at the age of twenty-one he became a salesman for a wholesale stationery company. About this time he developed a gradual paralysis of the throat muscles which threatened the loss of his voice. When the doctors were unable to find a physical cause for these conditions, hypnosis was tried, but failed to have any permanent effect.

As a last resort, Edgar asked a friend to help him reenter the same kind of hypnotic sleep that had enabled him to memorize his schoolbooks as a child. His friend gave him the necessary suggestion, and once he was in self-incuded trance, Edgar came to grips with his own problem. He recommended medication and manipulative therapy which successfully restored his voice and cured his throat trouble.

A group of physicians from Hopkinsville and Bowling Green, Kentucky, took advantage of his unique talent to diagnose their own patients. They soon discovered that Cayce only needed to be given the name and address of the patient, and was then able to "tune in" telepathically on that individual's mind and body, wherever he was, as easily as if they were both in the same room. He needed, and was given, no other information regarding any patient.

One of the young M.D.'s, Dr. Wesley Ketchum, submitted a report on this unorthodox procedure to a clinical research society in Boston. On the ninth of October, 1910, *The New York Times* carried two pages of headlines and pictures. From that day on, invalids from all over the country sought help from the "wonder man."

When Edgar Cayce died on January 3, 1945, in Virginia Beach, Virginia, he left well over fourteen thousand documented stenographic records of the telepathic-clairvoyant statements he had given for more than eight thousand different people over a period of forty-three years. These typewritten documents are referred to as "readings."

These readings constitute one of the largest and most impressive records of psychic perception ever to emanate from a single individual. Together with their relevant records, correspondence, and reports, they have been cross-indexed under thousands of subject-headings and placed at the disposal of the psychologists, students, writers and investigators who come in increasing numbers to examine them.

An approximate breakdown of the readings according to subject matter indicate that about sixty percent are physical diagnoses, twenty percent are "life readings," and the remaining twenty percent may be grouped under the heading "other." The "other" category includes readings on business topics, mental and spiritual themes, dream interpretation and a variety of miscellaneous subjects.

A foundation known as the Edgar Cayce Foundation, located at 67th and Atlantic Avenue, Virginia Beach, Virginia, was founded to preserve these readings. An open-membership research society, the Association for Research and Enlightenment, Inc. (abbreviated A.R.E.) P.O. Box 595, Virginia Beach, Virginia 23451, was organized in 1932 and it continues to index and catalogue the information, initiate investigation and experiments, and promote conferences, seminars and lectures dealing with these readings and related material.

Until recently the published findings of the A.R.E. have been available primarily to its members through its own publishing facilities.

Now a series of books dealing with subjects of popular interest from the Edgar Cayce readings are available through Paperback Library, Inc., and Hawthorn Books.

This volume deals with a portion of the Edgar Cayce readings catalogued as "life readings," particularly with those mentioning incarnations in Atlantis. These readings and the records surrounding them are some of the most controversial given during Cayce's remarkable life.

The life readings describing past lives in Atlantis as if they were experiences in early England or early America cover a period of twenty years between 1924 and 1944. They are the most fantastic, the most bizarre, the most impossible information in the Edgar Cayce files. It would be easy to present a very tight evidential picture of Edgar Cayce's psychic ability and the helpfulness of his readings if we selected only those which are confirmed and completely validated. This would not be fair in a total, overall evaluation of his life's work. My brother, the author, and I know that Edgar Cayce did not read Plato's material on Atlantis, or books on Atlantis, and that he, so far as we know, had absolutely no knowledge of this subect. If his unconscious fabricated this material or wove it together from existing legends and writings, we believe that it is the most amazing example of a telepathic-clairvoyant scanning of existing legends and stories in print or of the minds of persons dealing with the Atlantis theory. As my brother and I have said from time to time, life would be simpler if Edgar Cayce had never mentioned Atlantis. So, before others can point to these readings as unbelievable and impossible, here is the whole story. As the author has pointed out, there is a strange consistency within the hundreds of psychic readings given over a period of twenty years. They will take you back into prerecorded history to lands of myth and legend, and forward into a future of literally earth-shaking changes. Whether you are a science-fiction fan, someone interested in the psychic or simply one who enjoys a good story, you will find in the following pages a totally new account of man on earth and a new concept of his relationship to God and his fellow men. I must warn you, though, that if you persist in reading

12

this book you may never be able to return to our so-called "real world of facts" without the nagging suspicion that the fantastic events depicted just might be tainted with truth. Your suspicion may grow into something resembling conviction if Edgar Cayce's predictions for the next few years come to pass.

Names used in stories are fictitious, although the stories are based on actual cases. The number following a quoted or paraphrased extract identifies the reading from which it was taken, so that anyone so inclined may check the Edgar Cayce records at Virginia Beach for verification and further details.

Hugh Lynn Cayce

INTRODUCTION

Should an engineer jeopardize his professional reputation, invite his friends' scorn and risk public ridicule by writing a book supporting the legend of Atlantis? The answer is probably No, unless he happened to have been on speaking terms with Edgar Cayce and familiar with his work, particularly his life readings. I was on speaking terms with Edgar Cayce from my birth in 1918 until his death in 1945. He was my father. Furthermore, I have spent a great deal of time studying the records he left, especially the set of life readings concerning Atlantis.

First I should like to summarize the legend of Atlantis, and introduce the reader to the Edgar Cayce life readings and the theory of reincarnation. Only then will it be possible to understand the fantastic ideas and events depicted in the amazing Atlantis documents. The information from these readings has been arranged to the best of my ability in chronological order. Books, encyclopedias and newspapers have been scanned for discoveries that seem to confirm statements made by Edgar Cayce. Finally, the reader is presented with a summary of the information, together with my opinion of its importance to him in particular and to America in general. There are good—perhaps imperative—reasons why these data should be seriously considered.

Let us turn now to the legend of Atlantis, and the arguments for and against its Existence.

CHAPTER 1

The Legend of Atlantis

"Atlantis Believed Discovered But in Aegean Not Atlantic." So said a headline in the Norfolk *Ledger-Star*, July 19, 1967.

The same story appeared on the same date in the *New York Times* under the headline: "Minoan City, Found After 3400 Years, Is Linked to Atlantis."

Both stories refer to the discovery of a Minoan city, buried under thirty feet of volcanic ash, on the island of Thera in the Aegean Sea. In charge of the excavations were Dr. James W. Mavor of the Woods Hole Oceanographic Institute and Mrs. Emily Vermeule, Professor of Art and Greek at Wellesley College. Mavor and Mrs. Vermeule link their discovery with Atlantis because there is evidence that it was an advanced civilization and because it came to a sudden violent end.

Notice both headlines. The news value of this story is not so much the discovery, practically intact, of a city that flourished about 1500 B.C., but its possible connection with fabled Atlantis. This is the most recent attempt to rationalize the Atlantis legend by changing its location and date.

The oldest known mention of Atlantis is found in two of Plato's dialogues, "Timaeus" and "Critias," which date in the fifth century B.C. Plato introduces Atlantis in a conversation between Solon and certain Egyptian priests at Sais, as a large island in the Atlantic which sank in a volcanic catastrophe some nine thousand years previously.

Since Plato's time there have been hundreds of books

17

and articles written about Atlantis, most of these in the last two hundred years. Some try to show that Plato's story of Atlantis was not only possible but probable. Others try to prove Atlantis a myth, or else rationalize the story by associating Atlantis with some locality other than the mid-Atlantic and changing the date to a more recent figure.

A large portion of the Atlantis literature resides in the voluminous works of occultists of one variety or another and the unorganized products of eccentrics. It is the attention given to the Atlantis legend by pseudoscientists and cultists that causes legitimate scientists to avoid even discussing the subject.

Several medieval writers refer to this legendary land, but probably the best known and most popular book on Atlantis is Ignatius Donnelly's *Atlantis, the Antediluvian World*. First published in 1882, it was revised and edited by Egerton Sykes in 1949. No book published before or since has accumulated such a mass of geological, archeological and legendary material, nor presented so many ingenious and eloquent arguments in support of the legend of Atlantis.

Donnelly's arguments are based largely on evidence of similarities between the culture of ancient Egypt and the Indian cultures of Central and South America. On both sides of the Atlantic one finds the use of a 365-day calendar, the practice of embalming, the building of pyramids, legends of a flood, etc. Donnelly argues that both the ancient Egyptian and American Indian cultures originated in Atlantis, and spread east and west when Atlantis was destroyed. An Atlantean heritage, Donnelly suggests, would explain the fact that the Basques of the Spanish Pyrenees differ from all their neighbors in appearance and language. ("The Basque tongue is the only non-Aryan tongue of Western Europe"—*Lincoln Library* vol. I, p. 516). Similarly the Canary Islanders bear little resemblance to any African group and practiced mummification of their dead. Donnelly says Spain, Portugal and the Canary Islands would be likely landing spots for refugees from sinking Atlantis. He compares the names of cities of Asia Minor and those of Central America, cities which were already named when the first European explorers arrived.

ASIA MINOR	CENTRAL AMERICA
Chol	Chol-ula
Colua	Colua-can
Zuivana	Zuivan
Cholina	Colina
Zalissa	Xalisco

Such similarities Donnelly says, are too much to ascribe to coincidence.

Altogether Donnelly lists 626 reference sources. In spite of the flaws critics have found in his reasoning—he is accused of "reasoning from a molecule of fact to a mountain of surmise"—his was a monumental effort. His arguments make interesting reading even today and a worthwhile project might be undertaken, using modern techniques, to sift facts from speculations in his intriguing book.

Egerton Sykes, an Atlantean scholar who probably has the world's largest collection of literature concerning Atlantis, says there are actually thousands of books and articles on the subject dating from Plato to modern times. However, few writers have much to add to Donnelly's arguments. An article supporting the possibility of Atlantis appeared in the November, 1948 issue of *Science Digest*. This article, originally published in the *Technical Engineering News* of the Massachusetts Institute of Technology in June, 1948, reviews the best of Donnelly's arguments for the likelihood of a sunken island continent. It discusses the existence of terrain features on the ocean floor approximating those on land: i.e. mountains, valleys, plains with trenches and holes resembling rivers and lakes. Of interest is the fact that only a relatively small warping of the earth's crust (1/8000th of its diameter) could cause considerable portions of the ocean floor to rise above water and other land features to subside. Possible evidence that this has occurred in the past is detailed in this article. In 1898 the crew of a ship employed in laying submarine cable near the Azores was trying to locate with grappling hooks a cable they had lost in water about two miles deep. The jagged, rocky nature of the ocean bottom there presented difficulties and the grappling instruments had to be frequently cleaned of bits of matter. Here I quote from the article: "These particles of matter were found, on microscopic examination, to be lava, lava which must have solidified in the open atmosphere because of its vitreous structure. (Lava which solidifies under water assumes a crystalline structure.) Since lava decomposes considerably in 15,000 years the area below must have been above the water within that period." There is other more recent evidence for the former existence of land in the Atlantic. An article by R.W. Kolbe in 1957 (*Science,* vol. 126, pp. 1053-1056) reports the investigation of a deep-sea core taken from a depth of two miles on part of the Mid-Atlantic Submarine Ridge. His find of exclusively fresh-water plants (diatoms) in portions of the sedimentary materials offers evidence that this portion of the ridge was once above sea level.

O. Mellis, in 1958, in a study of the genesis of the deep-sea sands in the Atlantic Ocean, indicates that the sands of the Romanche Deep probably originated from weathering of parts of the Mid-Atlantic Ridge that once projected above the sea's surface.

And in a 1959 *Military Engineer* report, we find that "during hydrographic surveys by the U.S. Coast and Geodetic Survey sinkholes as large as ½ mile in diameter and 500 feet deep were discovered in the straits of Florida 14 miles offshore from the Florida Keys, where the ocean is 900 feet deep. They are presumed to have been fresh-water lakes in an area which subsided."

One of the best technical arguments for the existence of

Atlantis is to be found in "Ocean Bottom Investigations and Their Bearings on Geology" by René Malaise. This article appeared in *Geologiska Foreningens I Stockholm Forhandlingar* (Mars-April, 1957). Malaise argues that many of the terrain features of the Mid-Atlantic Ridge area, particularly the canyons on the ocean floor, could not have been cut by undersea turbidity currents but must have been formed when the present sea floor was once above the surface. He discusses ocean currents and their effect on the ice that once covered Europe and America ten to twelve thousand years ago. His article also contains drawings comparing flint points found in Sandia Cave, New Mexico, with Solutrean points from Morocco and France. The similarity of these flint points indicates a common origin. Since they are estimated to be twenty-five thousand years old, Malaise thinks their users may have spread east and west from Atlantis.

Still, none of these observations prove that Atlantis existed. At best they offer evidence that large portions of the bottom of the Atlantic were above the surface in the not-too-distant past.

From time to time a newspaper or magazine will carry an article or a statement quoting some authority as for or against the Atlantis legend. For example, the *San Jose Mercury* of July 17, 1958, quoted a Soviet physicist and mathematician, Professor N. Ledner, as saying he had spent twenty years studying the legends of Atlantis and was convinced that ancient historical documents and cultural monuments, together with recent scientific discoveries, show that such an island continent truly existed.

Yet, in spite of the efforts of writers such as Donnelly, Malaise and others to amass and connect archeological, geological and legendary material in support of the Atlantis legend, there is no scientific proof of the existence of Atlantis. Recognized remains of its culture and inhabitants are lacking. Myths and legends from the past, together with Plato's story, do survive to remind mankind of a bygone era. Some credible evidence is available to offer the possibility that "it might have been," but no evidence has been uncovered to prove beyond doubt that "it was." This does not mean that such evidence will never be discovered. But until it is, Atlantis is likely to remain a myth in scientific circles.

What of the other side of the coin? Is there scientific proof that Atlantis never existed? Actually, the greatest argument against the existence of Atlantis is the lack of any explicit proof for its existence. Most geologists concur with the concept of uniformitarianism, which implies relatively gradual change. They do not believe that any catastrophic events, such as would cause the sinking of a continent, have occurred in the recent past—the last ten to twenty thousand years. Some evidence is accumulating for definite, possibly drastic, climatic changes eleven to thirteen thousand years ago, but authorities are not in agreement concerning possible accompanying earth changes. The uniformitarian attitude is aptly expressed by Elizabeth Chesley Baity in her very readable book, *America Before Man*. Referring to the legend of Atlantis, she says, "It is not surprising that very little satisfactory evidence has been found, since Atlantis—if it ever existed at all—disappeared long before the memory of mankind, and at the rate normal movements of land take place it would have required millions of years for so large an island to subside into the depths of the sea."

You have only to read the chapter on Atlantis and Lemuria in Martin Gardner's book, *In the Name of Science* (paperback edition retitled *Fads and Fallacies*) to see why most scientists shy away from the subject. This chapter is full of shrewd, sarcastic comments on the theory of Atlantis and those who have written about it. Gardner's main arguments against the existence of Atlantis boil down to the fact that no reliable evidence, geological or archeological, supports it.

Other writers have attacked the Atlantis story from different angles. E. Bjorkman in his *Search for Atlantis* drew upon material from the Bible, the Odyssey and the writings of Herodotus, a Greek historian, in an effort to link Atlantis to an ancient Spanish or Portuguese city.

In *Lands Beyond,* L. Sprague de Camp and Willy Ley attack Plato's credibility through his contemporaries but fail to reach positive conclusions and end a chapter with this statement: "Just what Plato had in mind when he spoke of the Atlantic Ocean and the continent beyond is not quite clear to this day."

Even scientists in widely separated fields have felt compelled to make statements relegating Atlantis to the myth category.

The 1936 Spring issue of *The American Scholar* carried an article by E.D. Merrill (administrator of Botanical Collections, Harvard University) entitled "Scuttling Atlantis and Mu," in which he attempts by scientific argument to deny the possibility of Atlantis. He tries to show that there is no philological relationship between American and Mediterranean languages and no common domestic plants and animals in Mexico and the Mediterranean. His theme is that the development of agriculture in America paralleled that of the Old World but with a different series of plants. He says that most cereals, along with temperate zone vegetables and fruits, are of Eurasian origin, while most American species are of tropical or semi-tropical origin. He presents an impressive list of fruits and vegetables of the Old and New Worlds respectively. He argues that man entered America from Asia and that the high civilizations of Central and South America were developed without the influence of Atlantis and without intercourse with Europe and Asia. Merrill says that not a single common cultivated food plant or domesticated animal except the dog appeared in both hemispheres until after 1492.

This view, however, of non-communication between Europe and America prior to Columbus is not shared by all scientists.

T.S. Ferguson, archeologist and author, in his book *One Fold and One Shepherd,* presents an imposing array of facts to show similarities between the culture of the Middle East and that of Central America. The illustrations comparing seals, pottery designs, and architecture are convincing. In addition he lists 298 items of common culture. Admittedly, ideas and designs of a similar or even identical nature may originate quite independently in different parts of the world, but as one reads Ferguson's list of the number of different items and practices common to both the Old and the New Worlds, the possibility that all of these originated independently in both hemispheres seems rather remote.

Pages 22 and 23 of Ferguson's book contain an illustration of a seal dug up at Chiapa de Corzo in Mexico. Ferguson then quotes from a letter of Dr. Albright of Johns Hopkins the statement that "the seal contains several clearly recognizable Egyptian heiroglyphs."

On pages 49 to 52 Ferguson quotes Dr. George F. Carter, also of Johns Hopkins, as saying, "Some plants positively were pre-Columbian in the Old World and the New World. There is a formidable list of plants, most of them related to the Middle-American, Southeast-Asian areas that range all the way from probable to possible cultural transfers. The long-held doctrine of the absolute separation of Old and New World agriculture is no longer tenable—the plant evidence should be re-examined without bias."

Such statements, while they do not prove that Atlantis existed, indicate that there are certainly questions in the minds of scientists as to the origin of the high civilizations in South and Central America, and disagreements over the question of early plant domestication. The contemporary view is summarized in a beautifully illustrated book, *Ancient Arts of the Andes* by W.C. Bennett, sponsored by the Museum of Modern Art, New York, the Minneapolis Institute of Arts, and the California Palace of the Legion of Honor. Bennett makes this comment: "The problem of the migration of the earliest inhabitants of South America is a fascinating and puzzling one, but hardly more so than that

24

of the origin of the high civilization of the Andes. This involves the question of plant domestication and as yet the centers where the New World plants were first domesticated is far from established."

In the April 1949 issue of *Science Digest* another scientist in a different field, Dr. Maurice Ewing of Columbia University, has a short article entitled "Lost Continent Called Myth." Dr. Ewing is quoted as saying he has "mapped, probed, sounded and visited the ocean depths since 1935." He took undersea photographs as deep as 18,000 feet and "found no evidence of buried cities." His search was concentrated along the Atlantic Ridge running from Iceland to Antartica. At first glance this might be taken as proof against Atlantis' ever having existed, but a moment's reflection shows otherwise. Suppose the United States were wracked with earthquakes and volcanic action for a few months—or years. Our cities collapse in rubble, and are then buried under layers of ash and lava. Immense tidal waves sweep over the land, scattering and destroying any remaining structures and all evidence of man's handiwork. Finally the whole land settles under the ocean, and for thirteen thousand years tidal currents scatter and ocean sediment covers any residue of our civilization. In the year 14,967 someone takes a picture of a few square feet of the ocean bottom, or drills a four-inch hole in the sea floor. Do you think he will see any cities or core into an automobile, airplane or power plant? The chances are against it. But he would doubtless feel justified in concluding that America never existed.

The October 1953 issue of the *Atlantic Monthly* carried an article by Robert Graves called "What Happened to Atlantis?" Graves turns his attention to Greek myths and tries to show that the myth of Atlantis arose from the confusion of a Libyan disaster with the glory and demise of the civilization of Crete. He says that the Cretans converted a small island, Pharos, near the mouth of the Nile into a port which was one of the wonders of the world. The spectacular sinking of this island shortly after the destruction of Cnossus (a principal city of the Minoans in Crete) was united in legend with the traditions of a flood that caused the destruction of the Libyan people in Lake Tritonis (at one time a huge inland sea which today has shrunk to the Mareth salt marshes). These stories were handed down by the priests of Sais to Solon who embroidered the legends, thus creating our idea of Atlantis. However, the dates of the disasters cited by Graves are so much more recent than the date ascribed by Plato to the Atlantis cataclysm that one finally feels Graves' article, interesting though it is, is as full of speculation as any of Donnelly's arguments.

One of the most recent arguments against the possibility of a mid-Atlantic continent appeared in the October 21, 1961 issue of the *Saturday Evening Post*. In an article called, "The Spreading Ocean Floor," Dr. Robert S. Dietz advances a theory concerning the composition of the earth's crust and of a spreading ocean floor which he says would seem to preclude the existence of Atlantis. If as he says, however, the continents are only moving apart an inch or so a year, there would have been little change in the last ten to fifteen thousand years. Dr. Dietz is a respected oceanographer, but his theory may be only partially true. At any rate, allowing for drastic earth changes, there is sufficient time in the time scale of earth's history to slip in a continent or two in the oceans.

Finally, we seem to be going around in circles. The harder one tries to solve the problem of Atlantis the clearer it seems to become that no solution is possible. There is no convincing proof one way or the other in current literature. Until some written records of its history, other than Plato's, are discovered, or until some conclusive proof of its never having existed is derived, Atlantis is likely to remain a puzzle.

How is the legend of Atlantis connected with the Edgar Cayce life readings? As a matter of fact, unless proof of the existence of Atlantis is one day discovered, Edgar Cayce is in a very unenviable position. On the other hand, if he proves accurate on this score he may become as famous an archeologist or historian as he was a medical clairvoyant.

The 2500 life readings on file were given for approximately 1600 different people. About 700 of these people had incarnations in Atlantis that influenced their present lives—almost fifty percent of those who received life readings. However, Edgar Cayce did not mention every incarnation for each individual, only those incarnations that would influence them most in their current life, and those experiences that might be most helpful. It is not impossible, therefore, that almost everyone living today was in Atlantis at one time or another.

The amazing thing about this particular set of life readings is their internal consistency. Although given for hundreds of different people over a period of twenty-one years (1923 to 1944), they may be pieced together to form a coherent, non-contradictory series of events. Individual abilities and weaknesses are reflected in successive lives. When many entities who have lived together at one period of time again reincarnate in another era, group or national tendencies become apparent.

According to the Edgar Cayce readings, many individual souls (or entities) who had one or more incarnations in Atlantis are reincarnating in the earth in this century, particularly in America. Along with technological abilities, they bring tendencies for being extremists. Often they exhibit individual and group karma associated with selfishness and exploitation where others are concerned. Many of them lived during one of the periods of destruction or geological change in Atlantean history. If Edgar Cayce's prophecies are correct, a similar period of earth changes is imminent.

Unfortunately, few questions were asked about dates and seldom was this information volunteered. Only a few life readings give definite dates of occurrences in Atlantis. However, by correlating names and events in these with those in the undated ones, we arrive at a view, admittedly

27

hazy and incomplete in spots, extending far back into the unrecorded history of mankind. Instead of a continent destroyed in a single day, as related by Plato, we get glimpses of man's activity in a land wrecked by at least three major upheavals at widely separated times.

There are statements, which we shall examine in detail, that many changes have occurred in land areas (some having sunk, risen and sunk again) from the earliest dates mentioned (millions of years ago) to the present. There are some indications of disturbances about 50,000 years B.C. Another upheaval seems to have taken place at about 28,000 B.C., at which time the continent was split into islands, while the final destruction of the remaining islands took place about 10,000 B.C. It is this last destruction, I think, that Plato describes in his writings. Each period of destruction lasted months or years rather than days. In each case there was sufficient warning so that many of the inhabitants escaped to Europe, Africa, and the Americas. Thus, according to the Edgar Cayce readings, both of the Americas and portions of Europe have felt the influx of Atlanteans more than once in the unrecorded past.

Why does Edgar Cayce say that Atlantean incarnations exert so much influence on individuals, particularly in our time? He answers this question in a general reading given to provide material for a lecture on Atlantis:

"Be it true that there is the fact of reincarnation, and that souls that once occupied such an environ [i.e. Atlantis] are entering the earth's sphere and inhabiting individuals in the present, is it any wonder that—if they made such alterations in the affairs of the earth in their day, as to bring destruction upon themselves—if they are entering now, they might make many changes in the affairs of peoples and individuals in the present?" (364-1)

When we look at individuals who seem to have once been citizens of a country strikingly similar to twentieth-century

America, we often may recognize personal as well as national faults. This is the first step toward salvation, as is illustrated in the parable of the prodigal son (Luke 15:11-32. Note verse 17). Faults once recognized may be corrected, and America may yet be spared the fate that overtook Atlantis. At least some individuals may be able to change as Robert Dunbar did, and lead a creative—rather than a destructive—life.

What kind of nonsense is this? Is there any basis for such ideas other than in the imagination of Edgar Cayce? Let us turn first to the source of the information, and then see how it holds up in the light of recent discoveries. If it does, we will be able to look at the future through the mind of a psychic and try to glimpse our dubious destiny.

CHAPTER 2

Life Readings and Reincarnation

PART 1

Robert Dunbar's parents listened in amazement to their nine-year-old son.

Robert's face glowed with excitement and enthusiasm as he began to recount at dinner the results of his first afternoon's experiments with his new chemistry set. He had already performed practically all of the experiments outlined in the manual. His conversation was full of technical terms and the newfound thrill of putting various chemicals together. He was especially excited as he described how with just a few more ingredients he would be able to make gunpowder and thus create his own firecrackers and other fireworks to celebrate New Year's Eve.

The chemistry set had really been an experiment, for the parents were beginning to explore suggestions made in Edgar Cayce's life reading for Robert. This experiment was to lead the Dunbars into a new understanding of psychic preception and open for them the door into a whole new world of the theory of reincarnation and karmic urges from previous lives. Robert had seemed merely a bright little boy until they began to see him through the eyes of this reading. Now many of his talents, tendencies, and abilities began to form a new portrait.

William Dunbar remembered the day of his son Robert's life reading, and the funny sensation he felt when Edgar Cayce, speaking from a sleep-like state, charged him and Elizabeth with a grave responsibility in rearing the child. The reading described Robert's past lives in Germany, India, Egypt and the legendary country of Atlantis.

In Germany he was associated with an application of steam to move objects; in India he developed a combination of chemicals that produced explosives which were used against enemy tribes. References were made to electrical and mechanical work done with mathematical precision in other incarnations. The warning words of the reading rang again in his ears:

> *"for we find the abilities of this entity, especially, beyond the ordinary. Hence the necessity of directing [Robert] in the proper channels, that the world, the peoples, the nations may gain that advantage of the abilities of the entity. For turned in the wrong channels [his abilities] may become warnings to many that though they gain the whole world and lose their own soul, what has been gained?"*

This enthusiasm with the chemical set and the immediate attempt to make explosives was the first sign of the accuracy of Edgar Cayce's description of Robert Dunbar, but by no means the last. At an early age Robert developed an interest in cars and all mechanical apparatus. In high school he became interested in electricity. Encouraged by his parents, he went on to earn a degree in electrical engineering. He became interested in his life reading himself, and referred to it more than once during World War II, when he had decisions to make. Electrical engineers were sought for all kinds of assignments during the war years—some involved defense installations, others ways of dealing greater death and destruction to the enemy. Robert moved toward radar work. When Rommel's troops were overrunning Africa and an invasion of South America seemed imminent, Robert was busily supervising the installation of a radar network in the West Indies to protect the Panama Canal and the Trinidad oil fields.

At the war's end there were again choices to be made and these decisions were not always easy. In the fall of 1945 Robert wrote the following letter to his parents:

"Dear Mom and Dad,

"Today I had to make another choice and I hope you will think I did the right thing. The Colonel assembled all of us who are working here at the lab. You know I now have enough points to go back to civilian life; but they are pushing hard to keep officers in the reserve. There is a chance to stay in the army at my present rank with good chances of promotion, so the Colonel says, and transfer to Wright Patterson Field in Dayton, Ohio. The work is secret but I think it has something to do with missiles—some of the captured German scientists will be there and I am sure it won't be long before they tie that in with the atomic bomb. A country with such a weapon would be invincible. You know how I feel about the army, but there is another possibility. They are offering good civil service jobs to those with military electronics experience. It would be similar work, but as a civilian. This is much more appealing to me than the military deal and the pay is almost twice that of my old civilian electric power company job. The catch is the work is on destructive equipment, missiles and bombs. I read my reading over again and it is funny how I was sent to the Carribean near where Edgar Cayce said I once lived and where records may someday be discovered of Atlantis. This time I felt my work was constructive, not destructive. That is why today I decided against going into the missile program either as an officer or civilian. I hate turning down the good pay and a lot of my friends are going. They think I'm crazy to go back to an electric utility job and maybe I am, but at least it seems to be more constructive work. I am sure there will be a big demand for electric service once all the priorities are off and people start living like human beings again. I hope you both will think I made the right decision.

"Love,
"Robert"

32

Since the war things seem to have gone well for Robert. He hasn't gotten rich, but he has a beautiful wife, two fine children, his health and a comfortable living. I know Robert pretty well, since he is active in A.R.E. affairs, and once I asked him if he ever regretted not going on to higher pay and possible fame in another field. He smiled and said, "I've thought of it sometimes, but you know, most of the things I want I already have." I suppose few people today are happier than Robert Dunbar.

Contrast this story of constructive application of the readings with that of another young man. At the time of his first reading he was in college. The parallel between him and Robert was such that they might have been friends in Atlantis. Here was another individual with great scientific ability. Electrical and mechanical work was again suggested and again there were the stern warnings that his abilities should be directed in constructive channels.

The extracts from this reading have been paraphrased slightly for clarity. The reading opened by saying that "many individuals of unusual abilities—both for good and bad—were being incarnated in the earth at this time" (1910-1911). Mental ability, particularly, was listed as a characteristic of this person and the reading suggested research as an appropriate career. He was warned about his Atlantean incarnation, where he had used his scientific ability for selfish purposes, "impelling people to submit to another's will." His reading said that "if his abilities were turned to constructive purposes many would bless or praise him, but if turned to destructive or selfish purposes many will rue their association with the entity."

This young man, whom we shall call Tom, ignored the need for constructive use of his talents. He was quickly successful in the electronics field; the work seemed to come to him naturally. Tom became the director of a large electronics concern that made range finders for battleships. He was a pioneer in the development of a number of electronic devices involved in explosives and destructive equipment. During the war, Tom made a great deal of money. But it brought him restlessness and confusion, rather than peace and happiness. His problems cost him his fortune and his marriage; he had what amounted to a nervous breakdown. It was only after he turned to work in a more constructive area, specifically the production of extremely good electronic equipment for the entertainment field, that he regained his emotional balance and led a happier life.

According to Edgar Cayce, here were two individuals with very similar urges and abilities in the electronic and mechanical fields, acquired from an ancient incarnation in Atlantis. Each had choices to make. One moved in a constructive direction; the other, temporarily, in a destructive one. The former found fulfillment and peace; the latter discord, confusion and unhappiness.

According to Edgar Cayce's readings, this sort of thing is happening on a grand scale. Hundreds and thousands of people are being reincarnated now who carry urges from the once highly technical civilization of Atlantis. The problems they had then—selfishness, slavery and destruction—are being recreated like unfinished business to plague them again. These individuals are often extremists, with innate capacity for great good or great evil. How they meet their karma may well determine the future of our civilization.

PART 2

"Third appearance in this plane. He was once a monk." (5717-1, October 11, 1923)

According to Gladys Davis Turner, the stenographer who transcribed most of Edgar Cayce's readings, this cryptic remark is Cayce's first reference to reincarnation. When it was read to him after he awakened from his self-induced sleep, I am sure it was as much a shock to him as it was to the man for whom the reading was given. This man, who had secured physical readings for his nieces, was interested in metaphysical subjects, especially astrology. He had persuaded Edgar Cayce to try giving him a horoscope.

Between October 11, 1923 and his death on January 3, 1945, Edgar Cayce gave approximately 2500 readings dealing with past lives in the earth and their influence on the subject's present life. These life readings indicate that the will of the individual, together with influences from past incarnations, affect a person's present life much more than any astrological influences. Life readings generally deal with psychological problems and are most useful in vocational guidance and human relations. Deep-seated fears, mental blocks, vocational talents, and marriage difficulties are just a few of the problems explained by what Edgar Cayce called "karmic patterns" arising out of previous lives spent by an individual soul on this earth.

Karma, as he saw it, was a universal law of cause and effect which provides the soul with opportunities for physical, mental and spiritual growth. Each soul (called an "entity" by Cayce) as it re-enters the earthplane as a human being, has subconscious access to the characteristics, mental capacities and skills it has accumulated in previous lives. However, the entity must also combat the influence of lives in which such negative emotions as hate, fear, cruelty and greed delayed its progress.

Thus the soul is to make use of its successive rebirths to balance the positive and negative karmic patterns by subduing selfish impulses and encouraging creative ones. This leads to one of Cayce's most provocative concepts: the reasons for apparently "needless" suffering. For instance, one woman wrote:

"I have lived most of my life by knowing that the power of God would keep me alive and active. At present I am taking sulphur baths and massage to try to get well . . . right ear and Eustachian tube collapsed . . . lower colon stretched very large and small passage. Tired all the time. Use of arms slows my heart action and I become exhausted standing on my feet very long . . . Nerves down my legs hurt and pain, when I lie on them or stand.

"Why should I come into this life with such a broken physical body? It seems I have been through hell . . . and I have often wondered what I have saved myself for. I have always wanted to be of service to humanity, but have no strength—angina—pernicious anemia, etc.— since I was young."

This woman originally intended to get a physical reading (i.e., a diagnosis of her health and suggestions for improving it), but decided to request a life reading instead. The reading cited her actions in a particular incarnation as the reasons for her present suffering: *"The entity was a companion of Nero and actively persecuted Christians. That's the reason this entity has been disfigured in body by structural conditions." (5366-1).*

However, the reading told of other incarnations indicating spiritual development. The reading continued:

"Yet this entity may be set apart, for through its experiences in the earth it has advanced from a low degree to that which may not even necessitate a reincarnation in the earth. Not that it has reached perfection, but there are other realms of development if it will hold to its ideals—who would tell the rose how to be beautiful? Who would give glory to the morning sun? Keep the faith that has prompted you. Many will gain much from your patience, consistency and brotherly love." (5366-1).

In one of these a love of home and family, where even servants were considered and loved as part of the family, was mentioned.

This woman found in her life reading an explanation for her physical suffering and an incentive to overcome her difficulties. She applied this information constructively in her life. In answer to a follow-up questionnaire years after the reading she reported that since childhood she had had a serious back deformity which the doctors thought would be incurable and would eventually cause her death. It was always a great struggle for her to meet this condition. She also had lost a part of one finger at the age of four.

"Many accidents when young. Lost part of one finger. Hand mangled, but normalcy now . . . I am trying to hold a high ideal and help others to do the same. When we used to have a maid, she was considered one of the family. I am forever grasping at and striving for perfection, although falling far short. Have always hoped I would never have to live again.

"When in grade school and on through college, my parents never knew if I would live; was given up to die several times; but by will power I struggled on, not complaining but in constant pain. Medicine always seemed to make me worse."

The questionnaire asked specifically about the reading's giving her a Roman incarnation at the time of Nero: Did she feel that it might have been just as fitting if the reading had given her a Persian, Grecian or East Indian incarnation? She answered:

"When I was young, my mother wanted me to take music lessons . . . but I had no talent. At the end of a term, the music teacher dismissed me as a disgrace to her teaching. However, I learned quickly and easily 'The Ben Hur Chariot Race,' and played it on all occasions— so dramatically and fast that it shocked all listeners. When I looked at the picture on the outside of the sheet, with the charging steeds and chariots racing, with the Roman Arena filled with cheering crowds, I seemed to become as one with the whole living action—was aware of nothing until I hit the final note! At 57 I think I could still play parts of it, although I have not touched a piano for over 40 years. This was the only piece I ever learned to play."

This woman overcame her physical difficulties by will power, patience and prayer. Years later she wrote:

"Now I am almost the picture of health and younger looking than when twenty."

It is obvious, from her vivid descriptions, that this person tended to be dramatic. The casual reader might interpret this example of karma as God punishing the woman for her Roman sins. Although some karma may result in physical afflictions or extraordinary physical abilities, it is more often reflected in an individual's tendencies, aptitudes, or interests.

Many of these talents and tendencies, inherited from past incarnation, seem to crop up in individual lives. For example, in a life reading given for a girl five years old, it was stated that she had an incarnation in France where she was the equivalent of an interior decorator. From this experience, *the entity will seek a career. Even if she gets married early, she will still seek a career of some kind"* (1635-3). This girl also had an incarnation in Egypt at the time of Moses and Joshua and though then an Egyptian she was friendly toward the Jews. Besides compassion for the Jewish people, a tendency to travel was indicated. *"The entity will always be wanting to get on a boat to go somewhere"* (1635-3).

There has been a follow-up on this reading through correspondence with the mother. While nothing sensational was reported, it is interesting to note that as a little girl the child particularly liked to draw boats. Her mother was impressed by her involvement in a group discussion regarding the race question, especially the Negroes. She expressed her opinion very definitely on the subject, saying that she felt more sympathy for the Jews than she did the

Negroes, that the Jews had a culture comparable to any highly developed group, yet they were discriminated against. She personally knew Jews, she said, who were very superior people and yet they took discrimination for granted and did not fight back.

In her last year of college she started teaching second-year French in a high school where some of her students were only a year or so younger than she. She worked her way through college by doing secretarial work after school and in the summer. She commuted great distances, since the college, high school, her home and part-time job were far apart. Since college she has traveled a great deal. She went into civil service and became a claims representative for the Social Security Administration. The last report (March 27, 1967) stated that she is now an industrial specialist in contract administration in the Defense Supply and still travels widely.

There is nothing spectacular about this case, but there are interesting points that seem to tie in with her life reading:

1. Her talent for French.
2. Her feelings toward Jews.
3. Her desire to travel.
4. The fact that she sought a career.

Coincidence? Maybe. But remember that Edgar Cayce gave a life reading for this individual when she was only five years old!

I could continue to relate other life readings given for all sorts of people at different times in their lives. In a great many cases it is possible to show how these readings influenced individuals to change their attitudes, occupations and values toward more constructive lives. Certainly these life readings imply the existence of a soul, the survival of one's personality after death and the concepts of reincarnation and karma. However, I am not trying to "*prove*" these concepts, for a reason aptly stated in a reading given for a group of people who wanted proof of reincarnation:

"in giving that as we find may be helpful in such an experience, first they of the group should determine within their own mind WHAT is evidence; then be sure that is not evidence to thy neighbor. For we are not all of one mind and evidence or knowledge is an individual experience and must be experienced—what is proof to one will not be proof to another." (5753-2.)

This reading goes on to warn that knowledge not used is sin:

"Do not gain knowledge only to thine undoing. Remember Adam. Do not obtain that which ye can not make constructive in thine own experience and in the experience of those whom ye contact day by day. Do not attempt to force, impel, or even try to impress thy knowledge upon another—in the studies, then, know where ye are going. To gain knowledge merely for thine own satisfaction is a thing, a condition, an experience to be commended, if it does not produce in thine experience a feeling or a manner of expression that ye are better than another on account of thy knowledge. This becomes self-evident that it would become then a stumbling block, unless ye know what ye will do with thy knowledge." (5753-2)

That is, an accumulation of documentary evidence is not positive proof of reincarnation to everyone. With a wry sense of humor, the reading stresses the importance of striving to be a better citizen, a better parent, a better neighbor.

"For to find only that ye lived, died and were buried under the cherry tree in grandmother's garden does not make thee one whit a better neighbor, citizen, mother or father. But to know that ye spoke unkindly and suffered

40

for it, and in the present may correct it by being righteous—THAT is worthwhile. What is righteousness? Just being kind, just being noble, just being self-sacrificing, just being willing to be the hands for blind, the feet for the lame—these are constructive experiences. Ye may gain knowledge of same, for incarnations are a fact. How may ye prove it? In thy daily living." (5753-2)

It is impossible to accumulate evidence that will satisfy everyone. In the past some efforts were made in this direction. One enterprising investigator collected 124 cases of incarnations in early America. Of these she was able to dredge up—from court records, church records, old library books and ancient tombstones—evidence that might be associated with information given in the readings for fifty-six of the 124 persons. Although reincarnation is certainly one explanation of this correlation of material from the readings and historical facts, there are other explanations that would also explain the correlation. I am not saying such studies are useless. The accumulation of similar data from various sources pointing to the same conclusion cannot help but lend additional support to that conclusion. There is plenty of this sort of material available in the readings to keep investigators busy for a long time. In my opinion, however, some of the best evidence for the validity of the life readings, and incidentally, for the theory of reincarnation, is of a less direct nature. Suppose you take a number of individual life readings and extract from them statements dealing with something entirely different from the individuals concerned, statements dealing with history, geology or archeology. Suppose you find them to be accurate. Moreover, you discover that they give additional information that throws more light on a historical event, lends more weight to a geological theory or leads to a new archeological discovery. Again I will agree with the readings that for some people this still isn't proof. But at least it is a few more grains of sand in the balance that may one day tip the scales irrefutably in the direction of reincarnation as an accepted fact.

As examples of this sort of indirect evidence consider the following:

In 1958 a geologist, at that time a Ph.D. on the staff of a large, well known eastern university, read of Edgar Cayce and his work. That spring, during a vacation, he stopped by Virginia Beach, intending to spend a day or two at the A.R.E. looking at the purportedly remarkable psychic records. Upon reading a few life readings he became so interested that he spent his entire vacation at Virginia Beach. He returned that summer and spent a number of weeks doing research on these life readings, particularly looking for statements concerning past geologic events.

The results of this research was a scholarly pamphlet with the imposing title "A Psychic Interpretation of Some Late-Cenozoic Events Compared With Selected Scientific Data," published by the A.R.E. Press in 1959. This pamphlet has since been revised and expanded and the title shortened to "Earth Changes," but the conclusions of this geologist then and now are the same:

"Many of the lay and professional people who have studied the Edgar Cayce psychic readings have expressed an interest in knowing what sort of correspondence there might be between the geological and related material found in the readings and concepts of earth history which have been formed through scientific research. This pamphlet has been prepared for the purpose of briefly reviewing the correspondence that exists between the Edgar Cayce psychic data and scientific interpretations of earth changes during periods paralleled by the readings.

"Study of approximately fifty Edgar Cayce readings which describe past geologic events indicates that the information given in the readings is internally logical and consistent. Twenty of these readings, which describe events of earth history that occurred as early as Pliocene time (10,000,000 B.C.), are presented. The readings are compared to recent scientific information. Only a few of the statements in the twenty readings agree closely with current scientific facts; a number of them stand in contrast to present scientific concepts of earth history.

"Nine psychic readings are presented in this paper that treat current or future geologic events for the period from 1958 to 2001 A.D. The large number of catastrophic events that are predicted for this period are out of harmony with the standard geological concept of uniformitarianism, or gradual change.

"Most of the readings on prehistorical subjects were given in the 1920's and 1930's, and all were on file before 1945. It is thus clear that the majority of the psychic statements antedate nearly all of the striking discoveries recently made by such youthful fields of scientific endeavor as deep-sea research, paleomagnetic research, and research on the absolute age of geologic materials. *Whereas the results of recent research sometimes modify, or even overthrow, important concepts of geology, they often have the opposite effect in relation to the psychic readings, in that they tend to render them the more probable.*"

Another example of indirect evidence can be found in an extract from a life reading given in 1936. This extract has been paraphrased slightly for clarity:

"The entity was what would now, in some organizations, be termed a Sister Superior or an Officer of the Essenes. The entity ministered to and encouraged the disciples of Jesus, often coming in contact with the Master himself on the roads between Bethany, Galilee and Jerusalem. For the entity was associated with the school on the road above Emmaus near the road that goes down towards Jericho and towards the northernmost coast from Jerusalem. The entity met many of those who came seeking understanding of the teachings for the entity had

43

been trained in the school of prophets. In fact, the entity was a prophetess in that experience." (1391-1)

In 1936, this reference to an incarnation as a woman in an Essene community near the coast of the Dead Sea did not seem particularly significant. Eleven years later the Dead Sea Scrolls were discovered.

In 1951, ruins located exactly as described in this 1936 reading were excavated, uncovering the remains of an Essene community, now called Kerbet Qumran, where the scrolls were written before they were hidden in caves in the nearby hills. In 1936 no living person knew that these ruins, which were excavated fifteen years later, were an Essene community. Also, graves around Qumran contained skeletons of women as well as men. In 1936, some historical references to such communities indicated that they were composed only of men.

Here is another example, an extract from a life reading given May 6, 1939:

"For the entity was among those spoken of as "holy women," first the entity coming in contact with those activities at the death and raising of Lazarus and later with Mary, Elizabeth, Mary Magdalene, Martha; all of these were a part of the experience of the entity as Salome." (1874-1)

But the eleventh chapter of John describes the raising of Lazarus from the dead, and does not mention anyone named Salome being present. The Bible refers to a woman named Salome being present at the crucifixion of Jesus, however (Mark 15:40-41, RSV).

Here, again, an apparently insignificant statement from a life reading lay in the files for twenty-one years. On December 30, 1960, the Long Island *Newsday* carried an Associated Press Dispatch which described a find by Dr. Morton Smith, associate professor of history at Columbia University. Dr. Smith told about his discovery at a meeting of the Society of Biblical Literature and Exegesis. While studying ancient manuscripts at the Monastery of Mar Saba near Jerusalem, he found a copy of an ancient letter attributed to St. Mark, narrating a miracle absent in the present Gospel of St. Mark. Dr. Smith presented evidence that the letter was written by Clement of Alexandria, an author who wrote between 180 and 202 A.D. The letter incorporates the story of Jesus' raising Lazarus from the dead and attributes the account to St. Mark. Previously the gospel according to St. John has been the only one of the four gospels to incorporate the story of Lazarus. *A new witness to the miracle, a woman named Salome, also is introduced in the letter.*

The foregoing illustrations are not "proof" of the life readings or of reincarnation, but they certainly offer indirect evidence to substantiate statements made in these readings. The seeming insignificance of the statements thus verified and the time lag between the statements and their verification make them all the more thought provoking.

Most of the books written about Edgar Cayce have one or more chapters dealing with the life readings.* The first biography of Edgar Cayce, *There Is a River* by Thomas Sugrue, devotes the last third of the book to their effect on his life. In *Venture Inward,* Hugh Lynn Cayce describes their impact on his family from a personal point of view. Jess Stearn, in *Edgar Cayce—The Sleeping Prophet,* deals with predictions made in many of the life readings. However, there are two books by Gina Cerminara—*Many Mansions* and *The World Within*—that are based entirely on the life readings. Miss Cerminara's examples of individual and group karma based on Edgar Cayce's life readings are excellent, though they may prove disquieting. Another important book is Noel Langley's *Edgar Cayce on Reincarnation.*

* For the full bibliographic references of the books and articles mentioned in this paragraph and the following, see Appendix I.

As for the subject of reincarnation in general, there is a voluminous amount of literature available. Some idea of the theory's acceptance by a number of intelligent individuals may be found in *Reincarnation, An East-West Anthology* by Head and Cranston. Many of the world's great minds—Plato, Plotinus, Origen, Spinoza and Schopenhauer, to mention only a few—are apparently agreeable to the idea. Indeed, reincarnation is one of the oldest and most widespread beliefs about the soul. Two very readable, thought-provoking accounts are *The Case for Reincarnation* by Leslie D. Weatherhead, and "How the Case for Bridey Murphy Stands Today" by C.J. Ducasse. In his book *The Christian Agnostic,* Weatherhead, an English minister, has a chapter that presents an even stronger case for reincarnation than does his pamphlet.

Recently there was an attempt to establish a scientific basis for a belief in reincarnation.

In 1966 Dr. Ian Stevenson, head of the Department of Neurology and Psychiatry in the University of Virginia's School of Medicine, published a monograph with the cautious title, "Twenty Cases Suggestive of Reincarnation." He does not claim that his personal investigations have settled the matter. But his detailed scientific procedure is convincing. He relates the case of Imad Elawar, a five-year-old child in the village of Kornayel, Lebanon. Imad claimed to remember a former existence on earth in a village not far from Kornayel. Dr. Stevenson was present to personally watch and record as Imad first visited places and people he claimed memory of from a former existence. Stevenson impartially reviews various other possible explanations for the events he witnessed such as fraud, cryptoamnesia, genetic memory, extrasensory perception, personation, and possession. This case, as well as many of the other cases cited in Dr. Stevenson's book, suggests reincarnation as the best explanation.

The final proof, however, of any theory is, does it work in practice? And many individuals who had life readings are alive today to ask. Hugh Lynn Cayce, Jess Stearn, and

Gina Cerminara talked to these people, and found that their readings had a helpful influence on their lives.

Interestingly, it is not even necessary to have had a life reading to receive help from one. You may learn by example. In the fall of 1962 a half dozen young people gathered at an A.R.E. forum to discuss what just a study of some life readings had meant to them. Even though they had not received personal help in the form of a life reading, their attitudes had been changed by the ideas introduced in the readings of others. They looked at their personal problems in the light of reincarnation and karma. They applied principles and assumed attitudes in their daily living that Edgar Cayce suggested for others with similar problems. The results were impressive indeed. All reported they had been helped to a happier frame of mind and that many conflicts and much confusion in their lives had been resolved.

As the life readings in general can be used creatively, so can the ones dealing specifically with Atlantis.

CHAPTER 3

Atlantis Before 50,000 B.C.

"The earth was inhabited by animals long before it was inhabited by man" (364-6).

Rather a prosaic statement, and certainly in keeping with modern scientific concepts. However, other statements, particularly those concerning the length of time man has been on earth, were not in keeping with the scientific concepts current at the time of the readings. For example, consider these extracts from the Edgar Cayce readings given over forty years ago, about an incarnation:

"in the land now known as Utah or Nevada, when the first peoples were separated into groups as families. . . . The entity developed much and gave much to the people who were to succeed in that land, and in the ruins as are found in the mounds and caves in the northwestern portion of New Mexico may be seen some of the drawings the entity then made, some ten million years ago." (2665-2, July 17, 1925)

Another reading referred to an incarnation in what is now part of Egypt, though the land areas of the world were said to be quite different from the present.

"In giving such in an understandable manner to man of today, [it is] necessary that the conditions of the earth's surface and the position of man in the earth's plane be understood, for the change has come often since this age

48

of man's earthly indwelling. Many lands have disappeared, many have appeared and disappeared again and again during these periods. At that time, only the lands now known as the Sahara, Tibet, Mongolia, Caucasia and Norway appeared in Asia and Europe; that of the southern Cordilleras and Peru in the southwestern hemisphere and the plane of (present) Utah, Arizona, Mexico in the northwestern hemisphere [also appeared. . . .]

"Man's indwelling was then in the Sahara and the upper Nile regions, the waters then entering the now Atlantic from the Nile region rather than flowing northward; the waters in the Tibet and Caucasian regions entering the North Sea; those in Mongolia entering the Pacific; those in the plateau entering the Northern Seas. . . .

"The numbers of human souls then in the earth plane being a hundred and thirty and three million (133,000,-000).

"The period in the world's existence from the present time being ten and one-half million (10,500,000) years ago. When man came in the earth plane as the lord of that in that sphere, man appeared in five places then at once—the five senses, the five reasons, the five spheres, the five developments, the five nations." (5748-1; May 28, 1925)

In 1925 man's span on earth was measured in the thousands of years. The idea that man might have been on earth millions of years instead of thousands was considered not only incredible, but ridiculous. As we shall see, recent discoveries have pushed man's history back much further into the past. The information given in 1925 may still seem incredible, but certainly no longer ridiculous.

What evidence has modern science uncovered that might give credence to Edgar Cayce's ancient geography? Is there any evidence at all to indicate that man might have inhabited the earth as long as 10,500,000 years ago?

According to C.O. Dunbar's *Historical Geology* the area of New Mexico had developed its modern aspect by then, and caves as old as 10,000,000 years might be preserved to this day. The land-sea relationships of the rest of the world at that time have yet to be worked out.

On August 10, 1958, *The New York Times* carried an article in the "Science in Review" section entitled "Discovery of Italian Skeleton Suggests a More Advanced Human Ancestry." The article discussed the find by Dr. Johannes Heurezeler of Basle University, Switzerland, of a complete skeleton six hundred feet deep in an Italian coal mine. The age of this skeleton was established by conventional geological and anthropological standards to be 10,000,000 years old. Dr. Huerzeler lists several features that led him to conclude that the creature was a humanoid and not an ape. "It had a short face as opposed to the snout of an ape; it had no 'simian gap,' a characteristic space in apes between adjacent teeth and the canines; the front teeth are fixed steeply in the jawbones, whereas the front teeth in apes point out, the canine teeth are smaller than the big canine teeth in apes; the chin is rounded on the front instead of sharp; the nostrils are ascending instead of being flat as in apes; the lower three molars are characteristic of man and not of the apes; a hole that carries a human nerve through the lower jawbone is present."

Near the humanoid fossil were remarkable well preserved remains of ancestors of modern animals and plants known to be 10,000,000 years old, an otter, a large carnivore, two antelopes, a pig, a mastodon, and remains of an oak, laurel and gum tree.

Dr. Huerzeler's discovery was no mere accident. In 1872 a French paleontologist found fossil fragments of this humanoid creature in a coal mine region in Tuscany. They were then identified as an extinct type of monkey. In 1933 Dr. Heurzeler became interested in these fossil fragments and after studying the jawbone of one he became convinced that the identification as those of an ape or monkey was erroneous. In 1956, after twenty-three years of study, Dr. Heurzeler presented his findings at a meeting of the Wenner-Gren Foundation for Anthropological Research. Dr. Heurzeler found support for his conclusions in Dr. Helmut De Terra, then at Columbia University.

Working under a grant from the Wenner-Gren Foundation, a team of scientists headed by Dr. Heurzeler and De Terra searched systematically for twenty-eight months before they found the humanoid skeleton. They conclude:

"If man did have a common ancestor it was neither an ape-man nor a man-ape. It was a creature with characteristics of neither a man nor an ape, that lived at a very early age of mammalian evolution, possibly as far back as 100,000,000 years ago." At present, they said, "no one has any idea of what this primordial 'lump of clay' from which man and ape evolved looked like. All that is known is that it was not ape-like or man-like. What to look for is the next big problem. It will be not for a nonexistent 'missing link' but for a primordial 'lump of clay' from which incipient man and incipient ape emerged and went their separate ways on the road of their respective evolutions."

For a long time the oldest human relics known were considered to be those of Java and/or Peking man, estimated to be 300,000 to 500,000 years old. But even before Huerzeler's discovery, the *Miami Herald,* back in 1948, described the find of a Dr. Robert Broom of the fossil jaw of a giant ape-man near Johannesburg, Africa. In 1949 an illustrated article in *Life* Magazine about this discovery also mentioned the discovery of fossil fragments of a pygmy. The *Life* article also mentions the work of Dr. L.S.B. Leakey in Africa. Leakey continued in the news. In 1960 the *Cleveland Plain Dealer* carried an article about Leakey's discovery of "Zinjanthropus," the world's oldest human—age 600,000 years. Leakey had been searching the Olduvai Gorge in Tanganyika, Africa. In 1963 he unearthed bones of a different kind of ancient man which he estimated to be considerably older than the 600,000-year-old Zinjanthropus. In 1964 radioactive dating confirmed Leakey's estimate of ancient age and dated the find of these new fragments, dubbed "homo habillis," at 1,850,000 years old. In 1965 Leakey, at a three-day conference on "The Origin of Man" at the University of Chicago, presented his finds and announced the find of a third manlike creature called Pithecanthropine. Along with the bone fragments Leakey described the finding of primitive tools.

Another newspaper article carried additional details of Leakey's finds and described a new potassium-argon dating process that placed the bone fragments of one of Leakey's finds at 1,750,000 years old.

A more recent newspaper clipping (January 15, 1967) ran in the *Virginian Pilot,* (Norfolk, Virginia). It described Leakey's discoveries of the bones of a creature called Kenyapithecus Africanns and its age is estimated at 14,000,000 to 20,000,000 years old. The article mentions other discoveries by a Harvard paleontologist of an elbow bone estimated to be 2,300,000 to 3,300,000 years old.

In the January 1967 issue of *Scientific Research,* an article entitled "The Budapest Skull" describes the discovery of a fragment of a skull in a quarry west of Budapest by Hungarian National Museum archeologist Laszlo Vertes. The skull is believed to be a 500,000-year-old member of Homo sapiens—our own family.

Thus recent research and discoveries, rather than refuting statements made in Edgar Cayce's life readings, tend to render them more probable.

It is now being established scientifically that man is much older than previously believed—a fact stated over thirty years ago in a number of Edgar Cayce life readings. How does this relate to Atlantis? Where was Atlantis to begin with? To quote from a general reading given in 1932:

"The position . . . the continent of Atlantis occupied is between the Gulf of Mexico on the one hand and the Mediterranean upon the other. Evidences of this lost civilization are to be found in the Pyrenees and

Morocco, British Honduras, Yucatan and America.
There are some protruding portions . . . that must have
at one time or another been a portion of this great
continent. The British West Indies, or the Bahamas, are
a portion of same that may be seen in the present. If the
geological survey would be made in some of these
especially, or notably in Bimini and in the Gulf Stream
through this vicinity, these may be even yet determined."
(364-3)

The reading places the former continent or islands of
Atlantis in the midst of the Atlantic ocean, as did Plato. It
names the lands to which the inhabitants fled and the
places where one might look today for evidence of this
long-vanished civilization.

The answers to some questions in a later reading on the
subject of Atlantis provide additional information about
the earth's surface in those early days.

Q.6: *"Describe the earth's surface at the period of*
the appearance of the five projections."
A.6: *"This has been given. In the first, or that known as*
the beginning, or in the Caucasian and Carpathian, or
the Garden of Eden, in that land which lies now much in
the desert, yet much in mountain and much in the rolling
lands there. The extreme northern portions were then
the southern portions, or the polar regions were then
turned to where they occupied more of the tropical and
semi-tropical regions; hence it would be hard to describe
the change. The Nile entered into the Atlantic Ocean.
What is now the Sahara was an inhabited land and very
fertile. What is now the central portion of this country,
or the Mississippi basin, was then all in the ocean; only
the plateau was existent, or the regions that are now
portions of Nevada, Utah and Arizona formed the
greater part of what we know as the United States. That
along the Atlantic Seaboard formed the outer portion

53

then, or the lowlands of Atlantis. The Andean, or the Pacific coast of South America, occupied then the extreme western portion of Lemuria. The Urals and the northern regions of same were turned into a tropical land. The desert in the Mongolian land was then the fertile portion. This may enable you to form some concept of the status of the earth's representations at that time! The oceans were then turned about; they no longer bear their names, yet from whence obtained they their names? What is the legend, even, as to their names?

. . . .

"You see, with the changes when there came the uprisings in the 'Atlantean land, and the sojourning southward with the turning of the axis, the white and yellow races came more into that portion of Egypt, India, Persia, and Arabia." (364-13; 1932)

Note this reference to "the turning of the axis." Recent geophysical research has turned up the fact that the earth's magnetic field seems to have changed direction a number of times in the distant past. Currently this is attributed to a reversal of magnetic polarity, but no reason is advanced for such a reversal. Of course either the tilting of the earth's axis or the slippage of large surface areas upon a molten core would produce similar effects, but this idea has not seemed as logical to geologists as an unexplained reversal in magnetic polarity.*

The reading just quoted, like an earlier one, refers to "five projections"—as if man appeared on earth *in five places at once*. It seems to associate these five projections with the five races, white, black, red, brown and yellow. There is even a flat statement that these five projections happened at the same time and developed into the five races. There is no statement about how long this took.

* There is an article on this subject in the February 1967 issue of *Scientific American*.

Q.5: *"Did the appearance of what became the five races occur simultaneously?"*
A.5: *"Occurred at once."* (364-13)

Thirty-one years *after* the reading just quoted, the *Evening Bulletin of Philadelphia,* May 2, 1963, carried an article on the retirement of Dr. Carleton S. Coon. Professor Coon was curator of ethnology and professor of anthropology at the University of Pennsylvania Museum. The article mentions the scientific furor created by the publication in 1962 of Professor Coon's book *The Origin of Races,* which advanced a theory of *five separate races.* The article states that Dr. Coon believed "that man divided into five races or subspecies half a million years ago, *perhaps longer,* and the five races then developed almost independently. Homo erectus evolved into Homo sapiens, he believes, not once but five times as each subspecies passed the critical intelligence threshold. He suggests there may have been a time lag of as much as 200,000 years between the time the first subspecies became sapient (wise) and the time the fifth one did."

The answer to another question concerning these five projections opens the door to considerable philosophic speculation.

Q.4: *Why was the number five selected for the projection of the five races?"*
A.4: *"This, as we find, is that element which represents man in his physical form and the attributes to which he may become conscious from the elemental or spiritual to the physical consciousness. As the senses; as the sensing of the various forces that bring to man the activities in the sphere in which he finds himself."* (364-13)

As I understand this statement it refers to the five physical senses: sight, touch, hearing, smelling, taste. It sounds as if spiritual beings projected themselves into materiality, specifically to participate in experiencing these senses or sensations common to a physical body.

The Edgar Cayce readings certainly imply a spiritual creation and then the entering into the earth or materiality of these souls or spiritual beings. To me this is in accordance with the biblical concept of man's creation: "Then God said let us make man in our image, after our likeness" (Genesis 1:26 RSV), and "So God created man in his own image" (Genesis 1:27 RSV). Surely this refers to a spiritual creation. These souls or spiritual creations must have existed elsewhere or on another plane of consciousness while animal life was evolving on earth.

Some of the quotations that follow introduce rather interesting ideas about man's appearance on earth. Unfortunately no definite dates are given, but these readings must refer to a remote era. The particular quotations used here are intended to show that according to the Edgar Cayce readings, Atlantis was one of the places where man first appeared on earth in material form.

And here began the major problem that has plagued man since his advent into materiality—the use of his free will for selfish purposes in opposition to God's will. I am not at all sure of the period of time covered. From 10,500,000 years ago the readings next mention a date 100,000 years prior to an undated event.

"In the period, then—some hundred, some ninety-eight thousand years before the entry of Ram into India, there lived in this land of Atlantis one Ameilius, who had first noted the separations of the beings who inhabited that portion of the earth's sphere into male and female as separate entities, or individuals. As to their forms in the physical sense, these were much rather of the nature of thought forms, or able to push out of themselves in that direction in which their development took shape in thought—much in the way and manner as the amoeba would in the waters of a stagnant bay, or lake, in the present. As these took form by the gratifying of their own desire for that which builded or added to the

56

*material conditions, they became hardened or set—
much in the form of the existent human body of the day,
with that color as partook of their surroundings much in
the manner as the chameleon in the present. Hence
coming into that form as the red or the mixture
peoples—or colors; known later as the red race. These,
then, able to use in their gradual development all the
forces as were manifest in their individual surroundings,
passing through those periods of developments as have
been followed more closely by that of the yellow, the
black, or the white races, in other portions of the world;
yet with their immediate surroundings, with the facilities
for the developments, these became much speedier in
this particular portion of the globe than in others—and
while the destruction of this continent and the peoples
was far beyond any of that as has been kept as an
absolute record, that record in the rocks still remains.
Also their influence extended to the lives of the people to
whose lands they escaped. Even today, either through
the direct influence of being reincarnated in the earth, or
through mental effect on individuals' thoughts, they may
influence individuals, groups and nations in the present."*
(364-3)

According to Edgar Cayce the red race developed in
Atlantis and its development was rapid. Although the
previous quotations were taken from general readings on
Atlantis, there have been individual readings that refer to
incarnations very far back in the past and these too
mention some of the ideas touched on in the general
readings. One person was described as having been

*"in Atlantean land in those periods before Adam was in
the earth, among those who were then thought projections and the physical being had the union of sex in the
one body, and yet a real musician on the pipes or reed
instruments."* (5056-1; May, 1944)

57

Note the dates on the following quotations and how individual life readings given months apart in 1944 amplify a concept advanced twelve years previously.

"in Atlantean land when there were the separation of bodies as male and female." (2121-2; February, 1932)

"in Atlantean land when there was the first division of sexes among first offspring of such division, first of princesses of that period." (2753-2; July, 1944)

"in Atlantean land before Adam—timekeeper for those who were called things or servants or workers of the people—entity felt need of change or reform so that every individual would have the right of choice or freedom—felt desire to improve the conditions for worker—felt need of God's hand in what evil or Satan had brought in the earth." (5249-1; June, 1944)

Evidently, Atlantis was not all sweetness and light in those early days. Already there was a difference in consciousness among those beings that had projected themselves into material bodies. The following quotations seem to imply that these souls or spiritual creations began to project themselves into matter, possibly first as thought forms, then into more substantial flesh, probably for their own diversion.

"in the Atlantean land during those periods when there were the encasements and indulgencies of many that had put on matter or material bodies." (618-3; March 6, 1935)

"in that now known as the Atlantean land during those periods when the first of the sons of men coming for their expression into matter—and then it took upon itself the activities that brought destructive forces with those reactions during the experience when there were again and again the expressions of the sons of God coming into their manifestations in the earth through

58

taking on of the form of flesh in that experience." (866-1; March 23, 1935)

God's spiritual creations have now put on materiality, but probably not in the form as we know man today. The following two quotations may refer to the beginning of man as such:

> *"in Atlantean land when one individual first saw the changes that eventually made for that opening for the needs of, or the preparation for, the universal consciousness to bring into the experience what is known to man as the first created man—an adviser to those who would change their forms of activities or the attempts as later expressed as being rid of the appendages of materiality."* (2454-3; July, 1942)
> *"in the days when the sons of God came together to reason in the elements as to the appearance of man in the physical on earth's plane and this entity was among those chosen as the messenger to all the realm."* (137-4)

A general reading on Atlantis (364-4), compressing thousands of years in a few paragraphs, tells of early man developing rapidly there and speaks of achievements in electrical and aerial fields, particularly relating to transportation.

I would interpret the readings just quoted to mean that the thought forms, who once could move freely in a nonmaterial world (or a different kind of world than is experienced by our five senses), had projected themselves into material bodies. Once they had done this they were able to experience material sensations—heat, cold, pleasure, pain, etc. However, the more they sought sensual pleasure, through the gratification of selfish desires, the less able they became to move freely in and out of their material bodies. They became encased in them from birth to death and thus subject to all the laws of the physical universe. Evidently they continued to enjoy their material sojourn, and began to exploit the physical world and pattern it for their own pleasure and diversion. Reading 364-4 continues:

> *"but with these transpositions, with these changes that came in as personalities, we find . . . the Sons of the Creative Force . . . looking upon those changed forms, or the daughters of men, and there crept in those pollutions, or polluting themselves with those mixtures that brought contempt, hatred, bloodshed, and desires of self without respect of others' freedom, others' wishes— and there began, then, in the latter portion of this period dissentings and divisions among the peoples in the lands."* (364-4)

What the "sons of the Creative Forces looking on the daughters of men" means is subject to interpretation. I would interpret it as implying that the earth was proceeding along an evolutionary pattern (remember animals inhabited the earth long before man—there probably were man-like creatures) which was interrupted by the projection into materiality of these thought forms. It sounds as if they, in many cases, mixed with animals, the results being sometimes quite bizarre. A division of opinion arose concerning this mingling.

A quotation from Paul's letter to the Corinthians seems to me to echo this thought and point up the problems it created: "The first man was from earth, a man of dust; the second man is from heaven. As was the man of dust, so are those who are of the dust; and as is the man of heaven, so are those who are of heaven. Just as we have borne the image of the man of dust, we shall also bear the image of the man of heaven. I tell you this, brethren: flesh and blood cannot inherit the kingdom of God, nor does the perishable inherit the imperishable" (I Corinthians 15:47-50 RSV).

The reading continues:

> *"Then began that period when there were the invasions of this continent by those of the animal kingdoms. This*

brought about that meeting of the nations of the globe to prepare a way and manner of disposing of them, else they would be disposed of themselves by these forces. This animal invasion resulted in the development of destructive force as could be set and then meted out in its force or power. Hence the development of explosives that might be carried about, came with this reign, or this period, when man—or men—then began to cope with those of the beast form that overran the earth in many places. Then, with these destructive forces, we find the first turning of the altar fires to the sacrifice of those that were taken in the various ways, and human sacrifice began. With this also came the first egress of peoples to the Pyrenees. Later we find there was the entering into the black or the mixed peoples, in what later became the Egyptian dynasty. We also find that entering into the Og, or these peoples that later became the beginning of the Inca, or Ohum, those who builded the walls across the mountains in this period, through those same usages of that power that was developed by those peoples. With the same power those in the other land became the first mound dwellers, in that land." (364-4)

In spite of the awkward language used in the readings to describe these happenings, it is possible to decipher what was taking place. There is a reference to the use of explosives to combat huge and numerous animals which were threatening man's existence. There are statements concerning emigrations to what is now South and Central America, Egypt, Spain and Portugal. The next paragraph suggests the basis for some of man's early legends.

"With the continued disregard of those who were keeping the pure race and the pure peoples, man brought in destructive forces to be used by people that were rulers. These destructive forces combined with those natural resources of the gases, of the electrical forces made in nature, caused volcanic eruptions in the slow

cooling earth, and that portion now near what would be termed the Sargasso Sea first went into the depths. With this there again came that egress of peoples. Hence, we find in various portions of the world, even in the present day, some form of legend of these events referring to an 'Eden' of the world." (363-4)

Let us review this paragraph with the help of extracts from individual life readings see if we can piece together what may have happened during these early days in Atlantis.

First there were references to developing from thought forms to material bodies and allusions to aerial and electrical affairs as if there had been scientific development comparable to our own. "Atomic forces" were mentioned and means of transportation referred to. Later these scientific developments were turned to destructive purposes. The following quotations seem to refer to this period:

"in Atlantis before the first of the destructive forces; entity builded those that made for the carrying these machines of destruction that sailed both through the air or under the water." (1735-2; Oct. 16, 1930)

"in Atlantean land in first of periods as the people began to apply those laws as pertain to the combustion as made for the filling up of the skins that were used for those of transportation, excelled in use of the elevator in building in the earth." (1730-1; Aug. 14, 1930)

"in Atlantis before destructive forces arose—associated with communications, lighter-than-air machines, radioactive forces." (1023-2; Oct. 17, 1935)

These readings mention a period "before the first destruction." Note the mention of "radioactive forces" and the mention of what may have been flying machines and submersible craft.

A question in a later general reading on Atlantis asked

about the kind of people that existed then:

Q.3: *"Please give a few details regarding the physiognomy, habits, customs and costumes of the people of Atlantis during the period just before the first destruction."*

A.3: *"These, as we find, will require their being separated in the gradual development of the body and its physiognomy as it came into being in the various portions of the land, as well as to those that would separate themselves from those peoples where there were the indwellings of peoples, or man—as man, in the various areas of the land, or what we call world.*

"In the matter of form, as we find, first there were those as projections from that about the animal kingdom; for the thought bodies gradually took form and the various combinations (as may be called) of the various forces that called or classified themselves as gods, or rulers over—whether herds, or fowls, or fishes, etc.—in part much in the form of the present-day man (were one chosen of those that existed in this first period as the first destructions came about). These took on many sizes as to stature, from that as may be called the midget to the giants—for there were giants in the earth in those days, men as tall as (what would be termed today) ten or twelve feet in stature, and well proportioned throughout. The ones that became the most useful were those as would be classified (or called in the present) as the ideal stature, that was of both male and female (as those separations had been begun); and the most ideal (as would be called) was Adam, who was in that period, when he (Adam) appeared, as five in one —See?" (364-11)

These remarks remind us of the discovery of Leakey and others of the bones of giant manlike creatures as well as the bones of pygmies who lived hundreds of thousands of years ago in Africa. Also the gods and legends of Greek mythology are brought to mind. Is it possible that some of these myths and legends are older than we suspect? Maybe the satyrs, nymphs and other weird creatures of Greek mythology once existed?

A number of individual readings concur with the general readings on Atlantis regarding the idea of developing from thought projections into material bodies:

"in that land known as the upper Atlantean during those periods when there was the entering of many that took bodily form for the dispersing of the thoughts given by the lords of the land—entity used rather as the experiment in the associations with the various conditions." (2126-1; Nov. 17, 1921)

"in the Atlantean land when there were the first periods of attempting to use the creative forces for the separating of the influences in the activities that had come about by the thought forms and the activities of the creative forces of the Law of One." (1745-1; Nov. 12, 1938)

"in Atlantean land during period not of second destruction but of early upheavals and activities of varied groups that were a part of the evolution of bodies and minds and of the others that were a part of the idea of evolution for conveniences, for the settling of judgments, and for drudges in the activities." (3022-1; May 30, 1943)

Although given years apart, these individual life readings seem to refer to the same remote period of Atlantean history.

When the spiritual beings entered materiality for a while they were able to keep in touch with the realms from which they came. The following quotation refers to psychic communication with man's higher nature:

"in Atlantis, a priestess, a keeper of the white stone or that through which many of the peoples, before the first
64

destructions in Atlantis, kept their accord with the uni-versal consciousness through speaking to and through those activities." (5037-1; April 19, 1944)

However, as they became more enmeshed in materiality through self-indulgence they began to lose sight of their true nature—their origin as spirit. The following quotation repeats a phrase referred to before and indicates the beginning of man's involvement with sex—an involvement which has given him trouble to this day.

"in Atlantean land when there were those disturbing forces—or just previous to the first disturbing forces that brought the first destruction in the continent, through the application of spiritual things for self-indulgence of material peoples. These were the periods as termed in the scripture when, 'the sons of God looked upon the daughters of men and saw them as being fair.' " (1406-1; July 13, 1937)

The next two quotations introduce two phrases, "the Sons of Belial" and "the Sons of the Law of One," which occur repeatedly in the readings. They sound peculiar and awkward at first—but probably no more so than "Whigs" and "Tories!"

"in Atlantean land during those periods when there were the divisions between those of the Law of One and the Sons of Belial, or the offspring of what was the pure race and those who had projected themselves into creatures that became 'the sons of men' (as the ter-minology would be) rather than the creatures of God." (1416-1; July 27, 1937)
"in Atlantean land when there were the greater ques-tionings between the Sons of the Law of One and the Sons of Belial or between those that were purified by keeping of the pure strain and those that were projec-

tions by thought individuals or beings." (1417-1; July 30, 1937)

My interpretation of these statements is that some of the original spiritual creations or souls who had taken on materiality for their own diversion had in a sense become trapped in it. By misusing their creative powers in self-indulgence, they became subject to the laws of cause and effect—which include the laws of reincarnation and karma. These "Sons of Belial," as they were called in the readings, continued their selfish exploitation of the earth and its life forms until they lost sight of their true spiritual nature. This may be the real fall of man. A soul that has so separated itself from its maker by selfishness that even after death it can not comprehend its own nature but is drawn back into what it has created is indeed in hell. However, some of these souls (the sons of the Law of One) realized their predicament and attempted to create a vehicle (man) through which it would be possible for souls to regain a comprehension of their Creator. I believe these efforts culminated long after the destruction of Atlantis, in Christ, who voluntarily took human form to show man the path home.

A reading describing an early incarnation in Atlantis seems to affirm the idea of two divergent groups.

"In giving the interpretation of the records, we find that it is well that there be given something of the background so there will not be confusion. For in giving the experience of an entity's sojourn in a period as remote as the early destructive influences in that land called Atlantis, or in Poseidia, there is oft a confusion in the interpretations of the records as to whether Poseidia was the land or Atlantis was the land." (877-26)

Atlantis was a continent or very large land mass which was split into islands, one of which was Poseidia. This

66

reading also stated that Atlantis was only one of five places where man was developing as such:

> "There were also other centers that were developing. For in the projections they began as many, and in creating influences they began as five or in those centers where crystallization or projection had taken on such form as to become what was called man, though it hardly could be said that they were in the exact form as in the present."
>
> "So, in following or interpreting the Poseidian period or in Atlantis let it be understood that this was only ONE of the groups; and the highest or the greater advancement in the earthly sojourning of individual entities or souls at that particular period." (877-26)

Further on this same reading defines the Sons of Belial as those who sought

> "the gratifying, the satisfying, the use of material things for self, without thought or consideration as to the sources of such nor the hardships in the experience of others. Or, in other words, as we would term it today, they were those without a standard of morality.
>
> "The Sons of Belial had no standard, save of self, self-aggrandizement." (877-26)

In opposition to the Sons of Belial were the Sons of the Law of One, those whose standard was:

> "that the soul was given by the Creator or entered from outside sources into the projection of the mental and spiritual self at the given periods. That was the standard of the Law of One, but was rejected by the Sons of Belial." (877-26; May 23, 1938)

It sounds as if the spiritual beings who projected themselves into the earth life forms had creative power

67

themselves. Some misused this creative power to reproduce grotesque life forms for their own purposes, interrupting the evolutionary pattern going on in the earth. This did not begin immediately; several life readings refer to a period prior to this time:

> *"in Atlantean land before there were the definite separations of the children of the law of one and the children of Belial."* (1474-1; Nov. 11, 1937)
> *"in Atlantean land during those periods of early rise of sons of Belial as oppositions that became more and more materialized as the powers were applied for self-aggrandizement."* (2850-1; Nov. 14, 1942)

It was only after some became more interested than others in satisfying selfish appetites that a difference of opinion arose. For example, an individual life reading indicated that at that particular period this person lost spiritual ground

> *"in bringing servitude to many through the aggrandizing of those things that pertained to the gratification of material things, material desires in the body."* (1315-2; Jan. 26, 1932)

Another reading, *twelve years later,* gives additional details about this same period:

> *"in Atlantean land during periods when there were activities that brought about questionings that arose between the two great forces, the period before the first destruction of the land—among children of Law of One who cared much about those 'things' that were parts of the activity having been brought about by the great teacher in those experiences—entity aided in helping these to overcome, when they became aware of the relationships of the individual entity to the universal consciousness or God—periods of progression—entity*

68

lived to be 1000 years old in years as termed today—
saw many changes in the earth and in the way in which
preparations were made for the advent of the souls of
men to be brought to their relationship with God."
(3579-1; Jan. 20, 1944)

I think that the "things" referred to were the life form
creations of the spiritual beings who had projected
themselves into materiality. They may have been mixtures
of man and animal. Evidently they were held in low regard
and treated as slaves or machines. Actually they may have
been souls who had so indulged themselves as to lose any
freedom of choice they may have had and were deeply
entangled in materiality. One reading already quoted in
part goes on to describe these "things" and the controversy
surrounding them:

"Those entities that were then the producers (as we
would term today), or the laborers, the farmers or the
artisans, or those who were in the positions of what we
would call in the present just machines, were those that
were projections of the individual activity of the group.
"And it was over these then, and the relationships that
they bore to those that were in authority, that the
differences arose." (877-26)

The same reading goes on to explain what was meant by
"projections of the individual activity of the group."

"Then we find the entity, now known as or called(——),
was among the children of the Law of One; entering
through the natural sources that had been considered in
the period as the means of establishing a family.
However, they were rather as a group than as an
individual family.
"For those who were of the ruling forces were able by
choice to create or bring about, or make the channel for
69

*the entrance or the projection of an entity or soul, as the
period of necessity arose.
"Then such were not as household or as families, like we
have today, but rather as groups." (877-26)*

Another reading seems to refer to this same period of
time:

*"in Atlantean land when first upheavals were brought
about, when the activities of the Sons of Belial brought
to the daughters of the children of the Law of One the
abilities for enjoying the pleasures of excesses of every
nature in human relationship as well as those activities
related to same." (1999-1; Sept. 13, 1939)*

The preceding quotations describe the rise of two
factions, the followers of the Law of One and the followers
of Belial. (Webster's dictionary defines Belial as "a
personification of wickedness and evil."

Interestingly, there is a reference in some of the Dead
Sea Scrolls to "the sons of light" and the "sons of
darkness."

All of this seems to have taken place at a time "before
the first destruction of Atlantis." In fact, the dissension
between the two factions may have caused the first
destruction or contributed to it. The following reading
certainly indicates this:

*"in Atlantean land when there were those activities that
caused the first upheavals and the use of those influences that brought destruction to the land—among
those of the law of one but was persuaded by and with
leaders of the land to apply spiritual laws for material
gain—thus brought or aided in bringing what eventually
became the destruction of the material lands." (1292-1)*

Why are the ideals and purposes of these two factions of
70

ancient Atlantis important to individuals and nations today? The answer may be found in many individual life readings. Very often—in fact, almost invariably—individuals living today are associated now with a person with whom they were associated in the past to work out some unresolved problem. Sometimes the problem has followed the individual concerned through several lifetimes.

The following life reading illustrates this point very well. The suggestion for the reading was:

Mrs. C: *"You will have before you the life existence in the earth plane of (1968) born November 22, 1910, in Pine Bluff, Ark., and the earthly existence of this entity as Asmen-n, in Atlantis during the period of the first destructive forces. You will give a biographical life of the entity in that day, giving the development or retarding points in such an existence. You will answer the questions, then, as I ask them, concerning her present associations and the influences from that sojourn."*

Mr. C: *"Yes, we have the records here of that entity now known as, or called, (1968) and the early experience in the Atlantean sojourn as Asmen-n.*

"In giving an interpretation of the records of the entity, and in giving the characteristics or manifested personalities in the present, it is well that something of the experiences of life through such sojourns be put into words, [so] as to give a concept of the earthly experience during such sojourns.

"For the activities in the physical plane then would be hard to interpret in the terms of the experience of an entity living in the present. But, glimpse these—if it is possible in your own experience.

"We find that in those periods there was not a laboring for the sustenance of life (as in the present, but rather individuals who were children of the Law of One—and

71

some who were the children of Belial (in the early experience)—were served by automatons, or THINGS, that were retained by individuals or groups to do the labors of a household, or to cultivate the fields or the like, or to perform the activities of artisans. And it was concerning these 'things' about which much of the disturbing forces grew to be factors to be reckoned with, between the children of the Law of One and the Sons of Belial. For these were the representation of what in the present experiences would be termed good and evil, or a spiritual thought and purpose and a material thought or desire or purpose. Hence, the entity entered the experience as one of the children of the Law of One, or of the one purpose.

"The LIFE existence of the entity, as compared to the present, would be years instead of weeks; or, in that experience, to live five to six to seven hundred years was no more than to live to the age of fifty, sixty or seventy years in the present.

"Hence, to be understood, this must be considered in the mental experience of the entity in the present: There we find that the entity, as has been indicated, was PHYSI-CALLY in love with one of the children of the Sons of Belial. Hence there were disturbing factors. There was an attempt to influence the entity to refrain from associations with the children of Belial.

"For—compared with the present—the association would be that of a young girl with those who were given to debauchery, or to the satisfying alone of the appetites of every nature. These brought disturbing forces throughout the experience; yet there were the eventual associations—or conjugations—with the son of Belial. Thus there was the taking on of physical desires, the physical reactions which were at variance to the teachings and the innate expressions of those who had been the companions and associates of the entity.

"Hence there were turmoils throughout that experience, yet the entity in the whole sense never lost sight of, or

72

*sense of, the need for keeping the body and mind and
purposes in a correct, or direct, association or activity.*

. . . .

*"Thus we find in the present, the associations which
have come about with an individual who represented
that sojourn, or that one with whom the entity was
associated in that experience, there have come disapp-
ointments, and the not being satisfied innately in self
as to the perfect association, or as to there ever being
a perfect cooperative influence."* (1968-2; Jan. 25, 1940)

The reading went on with suggestions to this couple for
resolving their difficulties, stressing that determination was
required to accomplish this on the part of both parties
involved. According to Edgar Cayce, many personal family
problems are the result of past associations in other incarnations.

This does not mean that every family squabble can be
blamed on some past incarnation. But if reincarnation is a
fact and if we are usually associated with people that we
have known in past lives, it is likely that many problems
may be the results of our actions at that time. What is even
more important is that the manner in which we meet our
problems may well determine our future as individuals and
as a nation. Many individuals for whom Edgar Cayce gave
life readings were able to resolve many of their difficulties
and turn their efforts to more constructive, unselfish lives.
The future of our nation will probably be determined by
the ideals of its citizens and their attitude toward one
another. According to Edgar Cayce, many Americans
living today are influenced greatly by their previous
Atlantean incarnations. A look at what happened to
Atlantis—and why—may help us steer a safer course for
America.

Other readings concerning this early period refer to
scientific discoveries comparable to those of the present.

The language is not precise but it sounds as if a psychic in the early Nineteen-Thirties were trying to describe devices like lasers and atomic bombs that were not dreamed of at the time of the readings.

"in Atlantean land at the time of withdrawing from the Law of One—establishment of Sons of Belial—was a priestess in temple built in opposition to the Sons of the Law of One—during time when there was the creating of the high influence of radial activity from rays of the sun that were turned on crystals in the pits that made connections with internal influences of the earth." (263-4; March 6, 1935)

"in Atlantean land during those periods when there were the destruction or separations of the land during the period of the first destruction—among those who aided in the preparation of the explosives or those things that set in motion the fires of the inner portions of the earth that were turned into destructive forces." (621-1; July 21, 1934)

Thus man-made destructive devices triggered off volcanic eruptions and earthquakes. This resulted in the changing of the face of the earth. Parts of Atlantis were destroyed.

"in Atlantean land when there was the second division or when there was the destruction of the lands that made Poseidia the remaining portion in which there was the greater activity of the Sons of the Law of One. These periods when there was the application of much that is being discovered or rediscovered today, in application of power to modes of transit as well as use of nature's means for a helpful force in giving greater crops for individual consumption—period when a great deal of thought was given to conveniences of every kind." (2562-1; May 9, 1941)

"in Atlantean land just preceding the first breaking up of

74

the land when there was the use of many of those influences that are again being discovered that the Sons of Belial turned into destructive forces—could be benefits to communications, transportation etc." (2560-1; May 8, 1941)

Compare the last two readings, given in 1941, with the following quotation from the Encyclopaedia Britannica 1954 Edition (Vol. 2) under the heading Atomic Energy:

"At the close of 1938 O. Hahn and F. Strassmann had shown that barium, a medium-weight element, was one of the products when uranium was bombarded by neutrons. The significance of this discovery was communicated by Lise Meitner and O.R. Frisch, refugees from Germany to Copenhagen, to Niels Bohr who was preparing to visit the U.S. Arriving in January 1939, Bohr discussed these results with Einstein, J.A. Wheeler and others. The presence of barium meant that uranium had been split into two nearly equal fragments, a tremendous jump in transmutation over all previous reactions. Calculations showed that such a reaction should yield 10 to 100 times the energy of less violent nuclear disintegrations. This was quickly confirmed by experiment.

"Both Bohr and Fermi discussed this reaction called 'fission' at a conference on theoretical physics in Washington, D.C., on January 26, 1939, and Fermi made the suggestion that neutrons might be released in the process. If this were the case, and the number was more than one, some losses could be tolerated and still leave a neutron to initiate another fission of uranium, thus producing a chain reaction which would continue to burn uranium. This suggestion threw the meeting into an uproar while physicists who had facilities initiated calls to their laboratories to start the search for fission neutrons. They were found to be about 2½ per fission, though the number was kept secret during World War II.

"Work was continued in 1940 and it was found that the fission observed in ordinary uranium did not come from U-238 but from U-235, an isotope present in only 1 part in 140. *During 1941 experiments were continued and at the University of Chicago on December 2, 1942 the first sustained controlled production of atomic energy was accomplished.* It was a triumph of experiment, deduction and theory to which many scientists, engineers and technicians contributed."

Since the efforts to develop atomic energy brought advances in technology in many areas, the benefits to man gained as a result of the *by-products* of atomic energy development may well exceed those from the direct application as a source of power or explosive force. Now, as possibly in Atlantis, man has control of a force powerful enough to be a blessing or a curse.

Additional details of the first upheaval are found in this reading.

"The name then, was Deui (pronounced Dar, or D-R); and the entity was active in recording messages, and directing those forces. These were not only the rays from the sun, amplified by crystals, but were the combinations of these.

"For it was these gases, that were used for what we call today the conveniences as for light, heat, motivative forces; or radial activity, electrical combinations; themotivative forces of steam, gas and the like—for the conveniences. "Then this entity, Deui, was among those who attempted to make such influences a part of the experience of those who were—as indicated—the producers of food, clothing; for these 'human machines' as we would call them today (not the machines used for obtaining power from the crystals).

"The use of these devices by the Sons of Belial brought, then, the first of the upheavals; or the turning of the rays from the sun—as used by the Sons of the Law of One—

*into the crystal for the activities of same—produced
what we would call a volcanic upheaval; and the
separating of the land into several islands—five in
number.*

*"Poseidia, the place or the settlement of that particular
entity—Deui—at the time, then became one of these
islands. Hence the confusion that at times is seen by
those who would interpret such records." (877-26; May
23, 1938)*

Unfortunately, no dates were asked for or given to cover
the period from man's appearance on earth millions of
years ago to the first of at least three destructions of, or
land changes in, Atlantis. There are a number of readings
that seem to refer to the same event, a meeting of nations
to combat the animal life that threatened to overrun the
earth. A date is given for this meeting—50,722 B.C.—but
whether this is connected with the first destruction of
Atlantis is not known. The meeting seems to have been
held in Atlantis and scientific accomplishments, including
airships and laser-like death rays, are mentioned. One
reading mentions a "polar shift" that might have accom-
panied land changes.

*"in Atlantean land during those periods when there were
the first of the rebellions that brought the misapplication
of the knowledge; or the forces that might have been
used constructively but were used in destructive activities—entity joined with Sons of Belial who brought
about destructive forces in the attempts to destroy the
animal life that in other lands overran same." (1378-1;
June 1, 1937)*

A number of readings refer to a sort of world council
that was held to cope with the animal problem.

*"among those who came as messengers from foreign
lands when people planned to protect themselves from*

77

beasts of field and fowls of the air." (2675-4; April 15, 1926)

"in days when the peoples of nations gathered together to defend themselves against fowls of air and beasts of fields, came to meeting in lighter-than-air machine." (2749-1; May 13, 1926)

"in that land where people came as representatives of those who would make the lands secure against the beasts of the fields and fowls of the air or the animals of the air in the second rule in the Atlantean period." (2470-2; Jan. 21, 1926)

"in Indian land when Said was ruler—among those who gathered to rid the earth of enormous animals which overran the earth but ice, nature, God, changed the poles and the animals were destroyed, though man attempted it at the time." (5249-1; June 12, 1944)

"of that country to which messengers came when there was gathering together of men to defend themselves against beasts of fields and fowls of the air." (2855-1; May 29, 1926)

"in that land when there were gathering of nations to combat forces of animal world and kingdom that made men and men's life miserable, entity among those that stood for use of elements in the air, the elements in the ocean, the elements in the lands as applied to forces to meet and to combat those of the animal kingdom. Oft has the entity from this experience been able to almost conceive wherein the disappearance of those known as prehistoric animals came about." (2893-1; Aug. 13, 1929)

"—when Poseidian land was greater in power, when there was the meeting called for those of many lands to determine means and manners in which there would be control of the animals that were destructive to many lands. Entity in capacity of those who guided the ships that sailed both in the air and under the water, also maker of that which produced the elevators and connecting tubes that were used by compressed air and

steam and the metals in their emanations—especially as to things controlled by the facet for the radiation activity of the sun on metals and control of such and airships."
(2157-1; March 27, 1940)

Here are eight separate references to an event given in eight different life readings over a period of eighteen years. The *least* that can be said about Edgar Cayce is that when asleep he had a remarkable memory.

Due to the repeated references to this meeting specific questions were asked about it.

Q.13 HLC: *"Please advise me regarding the preparation and presentation of the article or story which I am preparing on the Great Congress held during the age of the destruction of the enormous animals that once roamed the earth."*

A.13: *"In the period when this became necessary, there was the consciousness raised in the minds of the groups, in various portions of the earth, much in the manner as would be illustrated by an all-world broadcast in the present day of a menace in any one particular point, or in many particular points. And the gathering of those that heeded, as would be the scientific minds of the present day, in devising ways and means of doing away with that particular kind or class of menace.*

"As to the manner in which these gathered, it was very much as if the Graf [Graf Zeppelin?] were to start to the various lands to pick up representatives, or those who were to gather, or were to cooperate in that effort. And, as this, then, was in that land which has long since lost its identity, except in the inner thought or visions of those that have returned or are returning in the present sphere, the ways and means devised were as those that would alter or change the environs which those beasts needed, or that necessary for their sustenance in the particular portions of the sphere, or earth, that they occupied at the time. And this was administered much in the same way or manner as if there were sent out from

79

*various central plants that which is termed in the present
the Death Ray, or the super-cosmic ray, that will be
found in the next 25 years."*

Q.14: *"What was the date B.C. of this gathering?"*
A.14: *"50,722."* (262-39)

This reading was given February 21, 1933. Twenty-five
years later was 1958. Again referring to the Encyclopaedia
Britannica, this time to their book of the year for 1958,
under the heading of Physics, we note two discoveries that
may relate to the statement concerning death rays.

"Following the discovery of the antiproton in 1955, a
group of experimental physicists at the University of
California in Berkeley began a systematic effort to
produce and detect antineutrons. They used the powerful 6,000,000,000-volt proton beam of the bevatron to
create a steady supply of antiprotons. They rea-
soned that it might be possible, by causing the antiprotons to pass through solid matter, to produce antineutrons, in the same way that protons were known to be
converted into neutrons as a result of collisions with
automic nuclei. The success of this scheme was announced in *The Physical Review* early in 1957 by B.
Cork, G.R. Lambertson, O. Piccioni and W.A. Wenzel.
With the discovery of the antineutron the following basic
symmetry law was confirmed: for every particle occur-
ring in nature there exists a second particle, called the 'an-
tiparticle,' with opposite electric and magnetic properties.

"With the discovery of the antineutron also came the
theoretical possibility of a source of energy hundreds of
times more compact than any previously existing.
Antineutrons could in principle be combined with
antiprotons to build up 'antimatter.' When antimatter
came into contact with ordinary matter all of its mass
would be converted into energy rather than only a

fraction of it, as is the case with nuclear fission and fusion reactions."

Another 1958 development even more in line with the idea of power from crystals is described later in the same article. "Along lines previously laid out by N. Bloembergen of Harvard University, H.E.D. Jcovil, G. Feher and H. Seidel of the Bell Telephone laboratories succeeded in constructing and operating a 'MASER' (Microwave Amplification by Stimulated Emission of Radiation). The amplification is achieved by storing up energy in a small insulating crystal of special magnetic properties. The release of energy is triggered off by an incident signal, so that the crystal passes on more energy than it receives."

The development of different types of MASERS is continuing today. The February 1961 issue of *Electrical Engineering* reports advances by I.B.M. on two new MASERS, or "lasers." Both permit continuous generation of coherent light waves for possible space communications and scientific and industrial uses. The April 1961 issue of *Electrical Engineering* describes a ruby optical maser and the December 1961 issue of the same publication describes a gaseous optical maser or laser. This latter issue also mentions work by Westinghouse on a project to convert sunlight to electricity by use of a thermoelectric generator. The December 30, 1961 issue of *Business Week* headlined "Laser Gun Shoots Light Rays" in the "New Products" section. Eight months later the same magazine features "The Laser" in a special report. Since then the technical literature has been filled with new laser developments. Lasers have tremendous potential in communication and thousands of other peaceful uses in measurement and control processes, medical instruments, chemical processing, cutting and welding and basic research. Obviously they may also have destructive potential as weapons.

A recapitulation of what has been brought out so far in the life readings covering Atlantean incarnations indicates that:

1. Man has existed in the earth for at least 10,000,000 years.

2. Atlantis was one of the places where man as such developed.

3. Man's origin was as a spirit, not a physical body. These souls projected themselves into matter, probably for their own diversion, interrupting an evolutionary pattern then going on in the earth. Through the use of his creative powers for selfish purposes man became entangled in matter or materiality to such an extent that he nearly forgot his divine origin and nature.

4. A very long time ago man attained great technological progress, equal to it if not surpassing that existing today.

5. Just as the misuse of their spiritual powers brought turmoil, strife and questioning among themselves, men's misuse of scientific and material achievements brought physical destruction in the earth.

At this point I want to refer you to *Book of the Hopi* by Frank Waters.* Frank Waters had the cooperation of Oswald White Bear Fredericks, a full-blood, college educated Hopi. Through Fredericks it was possible for Waters to converse with Hopi elders and to unravel the mysteries of the Hopi ceremonials which have baffled anthropologists and enthnologists for years. It is interesting to compare some of the Hopi legends with material in the Edgar Cayce readings. The Hopi creation myths link man to his creator through a series of psychophysical centers in the body. One is reminded of Hindu and Tibetan mysticism which postulates a similar series of centers of "cakras." A number of Edgar Cayce readings indicate a physical-spiritual connection through the ductless glands of the body, the pineal, pituitary, adrenal, thymus, thyroid and parathyroid, gonads and cells of leydig.

The First World of the First People of the Hopi sounds very much like that described by Edgar Cayce when man

* Viking Press, N. Y., 1963.

first entered materiality. The idea of a medicine man being able to diagnose one's condition by looking at him through a small crystal sounds very much as if the medicine man were seeing the "aura" or colored light emanation from a human body that Edgar Cayce often claimed to see and whose colors indicate one's physical condition.

The Hopi legends describe the destruction of this first world because the people "used the vibratory centers of their bodies solely for earthly purposes, forgetting their creator." The legend continues with a description of the separation of men and animals and the destruction of the first world by volcanic action and fire. Some people were saved by hiding in caves and eventually emerged to begin a second world. This second world of Hopi legend sounds like one of high civilization as "villages were built and goods traded." However, the more people traded, the more they wanted and they "soon forgot to sing praises to their creator and began to sing praises for the goods they bartered and stored." The people quarreled and wars began. The destruction of the second world is interesting, for according to Hopi legend the earth did not continue to rotate properly but teetered off balance and spun crazily around and rolled over twice. Mountains plunged into the sea and the seas sloshed over the land. The world spun through cold lifeless space and froze into solid ice. This brings to mind Edgar Cayce's statements of a shift of polar axis, and of course there is historical evidence of an ice age associated with worldwide climatic changes.

There is a Third and Fourth World in Hopi legend as well as the idea of the Hopi coming to their Arizona homeland from a country to the south. And these, too, as we shall see, relate to the Edgar Cayce readings.

CHAPTER 4

50,000 B.C. to 10,000 B.C.

A number of life readings refer to a second period of destruction which destroyed additional portions of Atlantis. During this time—evidently several thousand years later—there were great scientific advances. But friction continued among the people. To quote from individual life readings:

> *"in Atlantean land during those periods of greater expansion as to ways, means and manners of applying greater conveniences for the people of the land—things of transporation, the aeroplane as called today, but then as ships of the air, for they sailed not only in the air but in other elements also."* (2437-1; Jan. 23, 1941)

Communications and transportation were evidently as highly developed and as widespread as today.

> *"in Atlantean land when there were the developments of those things as made for motivative forces as carried the peoples into the various portions of the land and to other lands. Entity a navigator of note then."* (2124-3; Oct. 2, 1931)
> *"in Atlantean land when peoples understood the law of universal forces entity able to carry messages through space to the other lands, guided crafts of that period."* (2494-1; Feb. 7, 1930)

The three readings next quoted use an odd term, "nightside of life." They also mention "universal forces" "not of the present." Since the readings were given in 1928, 1929, and 1930, long before atomic submarines and nuclear reactors, I think *nuclear* power may be meant, for it is certainly a "universal force" and it may be used for man's conveniences or his destruction.

"in Alta in Atlantis, among those who were of the highest development in the material application of those forces as pertain to the nightside of life, or the ability to apply that of forces not of the present used in many ways for man's own use." (2913-1; Sept. 6, 1928)

Atomic power was not developed until years after 1928.

"in Atlantean land or Poseidia—entity ruled in pomp and power and in understanding of the mysteries of the application of that often termed the nightside of life, or in applying the universal forces as understood in that period." (2897-1; Dec. 15, 1929)
"in Atlantean period of those peoples that gained much in understanding of mechanical laws and application of nightside of life for destruction." (2896-1; May 2,1930)

The following references imply radio and television communication:

"in a land known as Poseidia, a musician in temple, sounds of all nature produced on instruments. Civilization materially higher than today; in position where worshipped by people in a portion of that land." (38-1; June 23, 1928)
"in Atlantis during higher state of civilization, teacher of psychological thought and study, especially that of transmission of thought through ether." (187-1; May 16, 1925)
"in city of Peos in Atlantis—among people who gained understanding of application of nightside of life or negative influences in the earth's spheres, of those who

gave much understanding to the manner of sound, voice and picture and such to peoples of that period." (2856-1; June 7, 1930. This reading, given in 1930, was well before widespread use of TV.)

"in Poseidia the entity dwelt among those that had charge of the storage of the motivative forces from the great crystals that so condensed the lights, the forms of the activities, as to guide the ships in the sea and in the air and in conveniences of the body as television and recording voice." (813-1; Feb. 5, 1935)

It is interesting to note the differences in dates, yet the consistency of the information, of the readings just quoted. They range from 1925 to 1941. As early as 1925 television was implied as commonplace in Atlantis at one time. This reading was given before television was commercially profitable in the United States. It is true that mechanical television schemes were conceived as early as 1884 by P. Nip Kow, and from 1910 to 1930 considerable work was done in the field of mechanical television. However, mechanical systems were abandoned in favor of electronic ones. The iconoscope was invented by Zworykin in 1923 and the dissector tube by Farnsworth in 1928. It was later in the 1930's before regular programs were broadcast.

Other readings continued to emphasize technical developments rivaling or exceeding those of our present civilization. Conveniences of all kinds were described; such things would naturally go with highly technilogical civilization.

"Had to do with mechanics, machinery, application of electrical forces, radiation and heating, commercial application; of same as would be called today." (1003-1; March 6, 1937)

"Name Lus-lu. Ruled as leader in city of Sus—interest in mechanical and chemical forces." (282-2; March 20, 1931)

"Excelled in mechanical appliances of period." (2122-1)

"in Poseidia when Alta in height of civilization—entity in service of country in relation to other countries." (This implies diplomat or ambassador. 234-1; May 20, 1924)

"in Poseidia, in decorative or art work." (4361-1)

"in Atlantean land at time of development of electrical forces that dealt with transportation of craft from place to place, photographing at a distance, reading inscriptions through walls even at a distance, overcoming gravity itself, preparation of the crystal, the terrible mighty crystal; much of this brought destruction." (519-1; Feb. 20, 1934)

"in Atlantean land before the second destruction when there was the dividing of islands, when the temptations were begun in activities of Sons of Belial and children of Law of One. Entity among those that interpreted the messages received through the crystals and the fires that were to be the eternal fires of nature. New developments in air and water travel are no surprise to this entity as these were beginning development at that period for escape." (3004-1; May 15, 1943)

The date of this statement is significant—it was not until World War II that the potential of the airplane as a vehicle for carrying heavy loads was realized. In 1944 the bureau of agricultural economics of the United States published the results of its experiments in the transportation of lettuce by air from the Salinas Valley in California to Detroit, Mich. and of fresh strawberries and tomatoes from various points south to northern cities. Since then, a wide variety of fresh foods has been shipped by air from western and southern fields to New York, Boston and other eastern markets. By 1950, scheduled U.S. air carriers were flying more than 100,000,000 ton-miles of freight and 80,000,000 ton-miles of express annually.

The following reading was given in 1933. At that time it sounded utterly fantastic and ridiculous. Today atomic power plants are in use and atomic fusion a possibility.

Advances in lasers and masers are coming so fast that articles describing them are dated by the time they go to press. The ideas presented in this reading are no longer ridiculous.

"As indicated, the entity was associated with those who dealt with mechanical appliances and their application, during the experience. And as we find, it was a period when there was much that has not even been thought of yet, in the present experience." (440-5; Dec. 20, 1933)

The next passage quoted from the same reading refers to the "firestone," or a device for producing power. It sounds very much like a fission or fusion process in which heat was converted directly to electrical energy. The application of this energy sounds as if the Atlanteans of the period had solved the problem of the wireless transmission of the power produced. This reading was given in 1933—before the development of atomic power plants, before the discovery of the laser and before anyone dreamed of a fusion process or the idea of containing hot plasma in a magnetic bottle. A layman today could scarcely describe our latest scientific developments any more clearly.

"About the firestone—the entity's activities then made such applications as dealt both with the constructive as well as destructive forces in that period. It would be well that there be given something of a description of this so that it may be understood better by the entity in the present.
"In the center of a building which would today be said to be lined with nonconductive stone—something akin to asbestos, with . . . other nonconductors such as are now being manufactured in England under a name which is well known to many of those who deal in such things.
"The building above the stone was oval; or a dome wherein there could be . . . a portion for rolling back, so that the activity of the stars—the concentration of

energies that emanate from bodies that are on fire themselves, along with elements that are found and not found in the earth's atmosphere.

"The concentration through the prisms or glass (as would be called in the present) was in such manner that it acted upon the instruments which were connected with the various modes of travel through induction methods which made much the [same] character of control as would in the present day be termed remote control through radio vibrations or directions; though the kind of force impelled from the stone acted upon the motivating forces in the crafts themselves.

"The building was constructed so that when the dome was rolled back there might be little or no hindrance in the direct application of power to various crafts that were to be impelled through space—whether within the radius of vision or whether directed under water or under other elements, or through other elements.

"The preparation of this stone was solely in the hands of the initiates at the time; and the entity was among those who directed the influences of the radiation which arose, in the form of rays that were invisible to the eye but acted upon the stones themselves as set in the motivating forces—whether the aircraft were lifted by the gases of the period; or whether for guiding the more-of-pleasure vehicles that might pass along close to the earth, or crafts on the water or under the water.

"These, then, were impelled by the concentration of rays from the stone which was centered in the middle of the power station, or powerhouse (as would be the term in the present).

"In the active forces of these, the entity brought destructive forces by setting up—in various portions of the land—the kind that was to act in producing powers for the various forms of the people's activities in the cities, the towns and the countries surrounding same. These, not intentionally, were tuned too high; and brought the second period of destructive forces to the *people in the land—and broke up the land into those isles which later became the scene of further destructive forces in the land."* (440-5; Dec. 20, 1933)

The next paragraph of the reading substantiates the idea that atomic power and radioactive forces were in use. It states that the same sort of force was used in treating individuals, which is what we do today with x-rays and radioactive elements.

"Through the same form of fire the bodies of individuals were regenerated: by burning—through application of rays from the stone—the influences that brought destructive forces to an animal organism. Hence the body often rejuvenated itself; and it remained in that land until the eventual destruction; joining with the peoples who made for the breaking up of the land—or joining with Belial, at the final destruction of the land. In this, the entity lost. At first it was not the intention nor desire for destructive forces. Later it was for ascension of power itself." (440-5; Dec. 20, 1933)

The next paragraph sounds like a description of a magnetic bottle for containing hot plasma or a giant laser.

"As for a description of the manner of construction of the stone: we find it was a large cylindrical glass (as would be termed today); cut with facets in such manner that the capstone on top of it made for centralizing the power or force that concentrated between the end of the cylinder and the capstone itself. As indicated, the records as to ways of constructing same are in three places in the earth, as it stands today: in the sunken portion of Atlantis, or Poseidia, where a portion of the temples may yet be discovered under the slime of ages of sea water—near what is known as Bimini, off the coast of Florida. And (secondly) in the temple records that were in Egypt, where the entity acted later in cooperation

*with others towards preserving the records that came
from the land where these had been kept. Also (thirdly)
the records that were carried to what is now Yucatan, in
America, where these stones (which they know so little
about) are now—during the last few months—being uncovered.*

*"In Yucatan there is the EMBLEM of same. Let's
clarify this, for it may the more easily be found. For they
will be brought to this America, these United States. A
portion is to be carried, as we find, to the Pennsylvania
State Museum. A portion is to be carried to the Washington preservations of such findings; or to Chicago."*
(440-5; Dec. 20, 1933)

I interpret this last paragraph to mean that some part of
a building or temple in Yucatan had an emblem, drawing,
or carving of one of these crystals (or firestones) on it.
Probably, in 1933, an archeological expedition was engaged in transporting portions of the temple or building
stones to the U.S. Possibly, even now, the carving or
drawing is reposing unrecognized in the basement of some
museum.

The description of the crystals and the idea of the
wireless transmission of power is not as fantastic now as it
was in 1933, when this reading was given. Recent advances
in solid-state physics have led to the development of
masers and lasers which amplify light waves, a form of
electromagnetic radiation.

Atomic power plants produce electrical energy. Atomic-
powered submarines cruise the seas. Experiments give
hope for the magnetic control of plasma that will make
possible the production of energy from the fusion process.
It has been proven possible to transmit a small amount of
power without wires.

Perhaps further advances may create a similar device
that can amplify and transmit larger quantities of energy.

Anyone familiar with atomic power plants and the
production of nuclear energy or with the construction and

operation of lasers will probably agree that Edgar Cayce's descriptions would do credit to a non-technical person today. That he was able to describe them to the extent that he did in 1933 is amazing.

At the height of this civilization there were statements about the misuse of power and warnings of destruction to come.

> "in Atlantean land during the periods of exodus due to foretelling or foreordination of activities which were bringing about destructive forces. Among those who were not only in Yucatan but in the Pyrenees and Egyptian land, for the manners of transportation and communications through airships of that period were such as Ezekiel described at a much later date." (1859-1; April 7, 1939. See Ezekiel 1:15-25, 10:9-17 RSV.)

> "in Poseidia—entity in household of peasant that gave information regarding the upheaval in the mountains that brought destruction to the land." (4353-4; Nov. 26, 1924)

> "in Poseidia when Alta ruled earth's forces—lost life in volcanic eruptions." (4219-4; Jan. 23, 1924)

> "in Atlantis when there were activities that brought about the second upheaval in the land. Entity was what would be in the present the electrical engineer—applied those forces or influences for airplanes, ships, and what you would today call radio for constructive or destructive purposes." (1574-1; April 19, 1938)

Evidently there was dissension among the people at the time of this second destruction as there had been during the first. The following reading refers to this dissension and also mentions atomic energy specifically.

> "in Atlantean land during those periods when there were those determining as to whether there would be the application of the laws of the children of One or of Sons of Belial in turning into destructive channels those

92

*influences of infinite power as were being gained from
the elements as well as from what is termed spiritual or
supernatural powers in the present. Entity wavered
between choices and when the destruction came about
by the use of those rays as were applied for beneficial
forces, entity misapplied ability—hence the influence of
atomic energies or electrical force of any nature
becomes a channel for good or bad today."* (1792-2;
Feb. 11, 1939)

Note the last sentence. This was a warning to a
particular person, but a similar warning was given to many
who had Atlantean incarnations, and with the atomic
capabilities of man today it is an apt warning for nations as
well as for individuals.

*"in Atlantean land in city of Poseidon when fires of
rebellion caused activities of those in high authority
that brought destruction to the land; in charge of
communication with Om and Mu."* (812-1; Feb. 4,
1935)

Since people knew of the coming destruction, many
made plans to escape to other countries.

*"in Atlantean land at time of second upheaval, coun-
selled those making exodus to other lands."* (1849-2;
July 3, 1939)
*"in Atlantean land during period of second disturbance
—among those persuaded to go to land of Mayra or
what is now Nevada and Colorado."* (497-1; Jan. 23,
1934)

An individual who, according to a life reading, had left
Atlantis at the time of the second destruction and gone to
what is now Peru, asked a question. This is one of the few
readings that mention a date.

Q.6: *"What was the date of the Peruvian incarnation as given in my Life Reading, and what was the disturbance in the earth as mentioned? Give such details as will clear up this period."*

A.6: *"As indicated from that just given, the entity was in Atlantis when there was the second period of disturbance—which would be some twenty-two thousand, five hundred (22,500) years before the periods of the Egyptian activity covered by the exodus; or it was some twenty-eight thousand (28,000) years before Christ, see? Then we had a period where the activities in the Atlantean land became more in provinces, or there were small channels through many of the lands.*

"And there were those, with the entity and its associates or companions, who left the activities to engage in the building up of the activities in the Peruvian land. For the Atlanteans were becoming decadent, or being broken up owing to the disputes between the children of the Law of One and the children of Belial."
(470-22; July 5, 1938)

Is there any evidence that man lived in North and South America this long ago? In 1951, newspapers carried an account of discoveries from excavations in the northwestern corner of Colorado. Robert H. Lister, Assistant Professor of Anthropology at Colorado University, is reported to have said that the stone and bone tools uncovered show that an Indian society existed there as long ago as 20,000 B.C.

On March 17, 1959, the *Virginian Pilot* carried an article by Joseph Alsop entitled "A Cookout in Antiquity". Alsop describes the discovery of the charred bones of a dwarf mammoth on Santa Rosa Island off California, by Dr. Phillip Orr of the Santa Barbara Natural History Museum, Dr. George Carter of John Hopkins and Dr. Wallance Broeckor of Columbia. Dr. Broeckor took some of the charred bones back to Columbia and obtained a radiocarbon date beyond 27,000 B.C. Alsop mentions other finds which have pushed back the age of man in America. There is the Tule Springs site with a carbon-14 date of 23,800 years ago. There is the Sandia Cave site, dated earlier than Tule Springs. Also mentioned were sites near Dallas, Texas of a camel-eating people. Tests by the Humble Oil Company laboratories dated these remains as 38,000 years old.

A United Press dispatch dated 1954 tells of a find near Sicily Island, Louisiana. A contractor bulldozing gravel in a pit thirty-five feet deep turned up pieces of leg bones, toe bones, part of a knee cap and several pieces of vertebrae. Dr. J.W. West, a geologist and curator of the Louisiana State University Museum, said the discovery may show that man was in this area as long as 50,000 years ago.

Going further south, *The New York Times* of July 22, 1960, carried an article describing the find of Dr. Juan Armenta Comacho, Director of the Department of Anthropology at the University of Pueblo in Mexico. His find consisted of a 4½" by 6" bone fragment dug out of the soil and gravel about sixty miles southeast of Mexico City. What is unique about this bone fragment is the carving on it. It contains crisp impressions of a primitive horse, a camel and a type of mastodon thought to have been extinct 100,000 years ago. The bone is dated at 30,000 years old. The date is confirmed by Dr. H. Marie Wormington, Curator of Archaeology at the Denver Museum of Natural History. To quote Dr. Wormington, "Only fresh green bone could take the kind of carving we find on this pelvic fragment. The carving could not have been done on fossil bone." The type of creature from which the bone came inhabited the area about 30,000 years ago. Along with the carved fragment Dr. Comacho found other uncarved bone fragments and stone tools such as knives, boring tools, spearheads, etc.

Since man is thought to have entered America from the Bering Straits, the find poses an interesting problem—that route was blocked by a great sheet of ice from 30,000 years ago until about 12,000 years ago.

Another interesting discovery was reported both by *The New York Times* on April 17, 1966, and *Science World* on April 15, 1966. Dr. Robert J. Menzies, Director of Duke University's Oceanographic program, and his colleagues were working on the research ship Anton Bruun off the coast of Peru where a great trench, the Milne-Edward Deep, furrows the ocean floor for six hundred miles. The scientists were looking for neopilina, a type of sea mollusk, one of earth's oldest "living fossils." Their dredges in this trench brought up some of the desired specimens, but their deep-sea diving cameras resulted in something unexpected —photographic evidence of what may have been an ancient civilization. The cameras had photographed carved rock columns resting on a muddy plain 6,000 feet under water. The columns were covered with what appeared to be some sort of writing. Nearby, the sonic depth recorder detected strange "lumps" on an otherwise level bottom—ruins of ancient buildings perhaps? The scientists are hopeful that further research will reveal whether a great city once slipped beneath the waves of the Pacific. Dr. Menzies hopes to revisit the area in a type of submarine now being developed by the Navy for deep-sea research. He is quoted as saying that although "the idea of a sunken city in the Pacific seems incredible, the evidence so far suggests one of the most exciting discoveries of the century."

Such discoveries are not confined to newspapers. The 1956 Book of the Year of the *Encyclopaedia Britannica* under "Archeology" lists radiocarbon dates for bones of camel, long-horned bison, horse and mammoth found near Tule Springs, Nevada, along with the tools of man (flints, scrapers, choppers, etc.). The age as determined by W.F. Libby is 23,800 years.

The 1957 edition of this same reference gives similar information for buried bones found on the island of Santa Rosa off the coast of California. The age in this case is 29,650 plus or minus 2500 years.

While not proof of Atlantis, these bits of bones offer evidence that man existed in the parts of the world, as indicated by the Edgar Cayce readings, as long ago as 28,000 B.C. Certainly recent discoveries show that man has been in the New World much longer than was previously believed.

We have looked at life readings relating to the "second period" of disturbance, or the breaking up of Atlantis into islands. The only date mentioned was 28,000 B.C., but a number of readings indicate great scientific development and migrations east and west to avoid the volcanic eruptions and other disturbances. We have found some recent evidence that man was in the earth at this time, even in the very same places Edgar Cayce's life readings mentioned. However, is there anything to indicate what kind of man he was or that he was anything but a savage? Is there any evidence for scientific development at that period?

New evidence about prehistoric man is found in Geoffrey Bibby's very readable book, *The Testimony of the Spade,* which deals with archeological explorations in Europe. Most people tend to think of civilization as starting with the Egyptians, and hitting high spots with the Greeks and Romans. They regard Europe as filled with barbarians and savages. Bibby leads his reader through numerous archeological investigations in Europe and comes up with a number of cultures extending back thousands of years. The fact that European history was not handed down to us in writing does not mean it is not recorded in many ways. Bibby discusses, among other subjects, the cave paintings at Lascaux and Altamira. These caves of Southern France and Spain contain remarkable paintings showing a high degree of artistic ability. Estimates of their age range from 15,000 to 30,000 years. They are attributed to Cro-Magnon man. Cro-Magnon man was not ape-like. Bibby says, "Skull capacity was above modern man. He was about 6'6" tall with high forehead, prominent cheek bones and a firm chin. *If he is an ancestor of modern man there would appear to have been a process of degeneration from that point to the present day."*

Remember references to the Pyrenees in the life readings? Could Cro-Magnon men have been refugees from Atlàntis?

The baffling and thought-provoking case of the Piri Reis Maps indicates that scientifically advanced civilizations existed in prehistoric eras. The story of the maps was brought to the attention of the public on August 26, 1956, in a radio broadcast by the Georgetown University Forum, Washington, D.C.* Participating in the broadcast were:

Rev. Daniel Linehan, S.S.—Director of Western Observatory of Boston College, seismologist, and a participant in recent U.S. Navy explorations in Antartica.
Mr. A.H. Mallery—well-known authority on ancient maps. It was he who "discovered" these maps in the Library of Congress and solved their projection.
Mr. I.I. Walters—Cartographer, formerly with the U.S. Hydrographic office.

Piri Reis was a Turkish admiral and geographer of the sixteenth century, whose pilot and slave had been on voyages with Columbus. When captured, the pilot had with him a map used by Columbus. Using this and other ancient Greek maps (handed down from the time of Alexander the Great) Piri Reis compiled a world map which shows the coasts of South America, Africa and a portion of Antartica. Interestingly, the section of Antartica is shown in an unglaciated condition. Evidently the surveyors who made the original map from which Piri Reis copied his map had performed their survey thousands of years ago, before the land was covered with ice. Even more interesting, Rev. Daniel Linehan, who had conducted seismic surveys in the

* A transcript of the broadcast is in the A.R.E. files at Virginia Beach.

Antartic, confirms the amazing accuracy of these ancient maps. Mr. Walters also confirmed the accuracy of Mr. Mallery's ancient maps and said that some of the maps showed mountain ranges in Canada and Alaska that the Army map service once did not have but which have since been found. They also record accurately the sub-glacial topography of Greenland. The statement was made in the broadcast that it would seem impossible for such a mapping feat to have been accomplished *without the aid of aerial surveys*.

Were the Piri Reis maps copies of older maps made by the Atlanteans with airplanes? Is this another link in the chain of evidence supporting the Edgar Cayce life readings, a chain growing stronger, not weaker, with scientific discoveries in various fields?

Along with their scientific achievements the Atlanteans had their social problems. The same terms, "Sons of the Law of One" and "Sons of Belial" are used to describe the opposing factions. The basic cause of the friction between the two groups was the same as it had been in the past—selfishness—and the same as it is today.

The following quotations are taken from five readings some of which were given eleven years apart. Each relates a different aspect of what was happening at the time, but the time itself is fixed by a reference to this being "before the second destruction" or before the upheavals that separated the large land mass into islands.

"in Atlantis before the second upheavals, a priestess in the temple through which mystics studied those tenets of the application of spiritual laws to material things." (3479-2; March 21, 1944)
"in Atlantean land prior to second upheavals—one sympathetic to lowly workers." (1626-1; June 29, 1938)
"in Atlantis before second breaking up of the land—

99

used divine force for gratifying selfish appetites." (3633-1; Jan. 25, 1944)

"in Atlantean land during period of changing of individuals from double sex or the abilities of progeneration of activities of self—priestess just before the activities of Sons of Belial that brought about period of second destruction; entity aided common people, its consideration brought about worshipfulness to the entity." (2390-1; Nov. 2, 1940)

"in Atlantean land before period of second turmoils that separated land into islands, in city of Eden in Poseidia among Atlan lands and people during building of temple of Law of One." (390-2; Aug. 15, 1933)

A number of other life readings, also given months and years apart, may be pieced together to glimpse what occurred during this second period of destruction. Whichever group may be blamed for setting in motion forces that led to the ensuing destruction, both suffered.

"in Atlantean land during second of destructive forces that brought destruction to those of one faith and to those of Belial, a brother of prince of Atlantis whose name was Atlan." (416-1; Oct. 8, 1933)

"At the time when rebellious forces disputed the acts and laws pertaining to the communication with what is termed in the present 'unseen forces.' Entity saw upheavals from destructive forces from the prisms, activities that brought fires to the surface from nature's storehouse." (820-1; Feb. 8, 1935)

This reference to "prisms" probably refers to the "crystals" described in other readings. The description of these crystals sounds as if Edgar Cayce was trying to describe what is known today as a laser or maser.

The next few quotations from individual readings given years apart confirm and amplify statements in other readings such as:

100

1. During this second period of destruction the Atlantean land mass was divided into islands.

2. Strife between groups characterized or even brought on this destruction.

3. Much of the discord centered around the attitudes towards the "things" or those of low estate.

"in Atlantean land when turmoils and strife arose from rejections of tenets of Law of One, and there was egress from that city of the Poseidian land when upheavals began." (813-1; Feb. 5, 1935)

"in Atlantean land when rebellions brought about separation in the isles and upheavals in the lands—aided in bringing the beauties of life as well as necessities to peoples." (441-1; Nov. 14, 1933)

The next two quotations are from readings given ten years apart. The phraseology is different but they probably refer to incarnations near the same period of time. Certainly they refer to the same problem.

"Of upper classes in Poseidian land, belittled self for better understanding between those that ruled and those that supplied necessities." (280-1; Feb. 22, 1933)

"in Atlantean land during period of disturbances between Sons of Belial and Sons of Law of One, one of priests creating better conditions for the 'things' or those used as laboring people in those periods." (3034-1; May 28, 1943)

The following reading probably also refers to the same era.

"in Atlantean land when there were those disturbances due to confusion arising between those in authority that would make for the universality of knowledge of all nature and those that held for caste or position." (1302-2; Dec. 22, 1936)

These readings indicate dissensions caused by social problems. The reference to the "things" imply that these creations probably had the status of slaves and were treated more like slaves or robots than human beings. Evidently one group, the Sons of Belial, wanted to keep these creatures in a state of slavery, while the other group (the Sons of the Law of One) wanted to treat these creatures like the entrapped souls they were and help them regain a comprehension of their relationship with God.

Some of the readings become quite specific about the problems.

"in Atlantis when there were turmoils between children of Law of One and Sons of Belial, found Sons of Belial desirable for gratification of material emotions and desires." (3376-2; Nov. 22, 1943)

At this point it might be well to quote from a reading that not only indicates a high development of psychic ability at this period of Atlantean history, but gives more details on the warring factions of that long-ago age. Also in this reading are statements regarding those who had pushed themselves into matter for self-gratification only, who had lost self-control and become as "things." Edgar Cayce began the reading by saying:

"In giving the interpretation of the records, or a biographical interpretation of the experiences of the entity during the Atlantean sojourn, something of the history and conditions at the time should be comprehended—if the interpretation is to be in terms of present-day experiences.

"Through that particular period of experiences in Atlantis, the children of the Law of One—including this entity, Rhea, as the high priestess—were giving periods to the concentration of thought for the use of the universal forces, through the guidance or direction of the saints (as would be termed today).

"There are few terms in the present that would indicate the state of consciousness; save that, through the concentration of the group mind of the children of the Law of One, they entered into a fourth-dimensional consciousness—or were absent from the body." (2464-2)

The reading goes on to indicate that such group meditation, prayer or concentration together promoted knowledge and understanding within the group. It sounds as if such activity resulted in a sort of tapping of the subconscious and using powers of the mind not normally used in the conscious state. The same reading later refers to those who used

"individuals and material things for self-aggrandizement or indulgence without due consideration for the freedom of choice or decision by those who were then, in a physical experience, in that state of evolution of developing their mental abilities for single or separate activity." (2464-2)

Later on, the reading describes something of the consciousness of the individuals in that state of evolution or development referred to as "things."

"Those individuals who had through their sojourns in the earth as souls pushed into matter as to become separate entities, without the consideration of principle or the ability of self-control, might be compared to the domestic pets of today—as the present development of the horse, the mule, the dog, the cat.
"This is NOT intended to indicate that there is transmigration or transmutation of the soul from animal to human; but the comparison is made as to trait, as to mind, as to how those so domesticated in the present are dependent upon their masters for that consideration of their material as well as mental welfare—yet in each

*there is still the instinct, the predominant nature of that
class or group-soul impregnation into which it has
pushed itself for self-expression."* (2464-2; Nov. 13,
1941)

Evidently some wanted to keep these creatures in their
place as slaves or robots to be used for their own pleasure
and convenience while others wanted to see them develop
to higher states of consciousness. Disputes arose over
whether these "things" were to be exploited or to be made
equals with those endowed with spiritual understanding.

The preceding reading gives a further explanation of the
difference in attitude of the "Sons of the Law of One" and
the "Sons of Belial," a difference that we might summarize
today as like that between "those who follow Christ" and
"those who follow self." The following paragraph, which
was also in this reading, states that these same problems
remain to this day.

*"For, as it remains in the present day: That declaration
made and those influences entertained, whether for construction or destruction, depend upon the spirit with
which the declaration was made.*
*"In other words, with what spirit do ye declare thyself?
That in conformity with the universal consciousness, the
law of love? Or that of hate, dissension, contention—
which brings or produce burdens upon thy fellow
associates?*
*"For the law of love is unchangeable; in that as ye do it
to the least of thy fellows, ye do it to thy Maker."* (2464-
2; Nov. 13, 1941)

The three readings next quoted amplify the concepts just
described. Also they are very characteristic of the consistency of the Edgar Cayce data. One was given in January of 1944, one in June of 1944, and one ten years
previously. Yet they so obviously refer to the same period
of time in Atlantis that they might have been given ten

minutes apart. It is this consistency that lends authenticity to the amazing data that poured from Edgar Cayce's subconscious.

"in Atlantis during what was known as the second breaking up of the land [the entity was] among children of Law of One, yet embraced many activities of Sons of Belial. As bidden by ones in authority there should be little mixing of groups in efforts to establish, to use offspring as beasts of burden, or workers in clay or in mills." (5245-1; June 3, 1944)

"a priest of the Law of One pitted self against many of those things that were presented by a people that were being drawn gradually into self-indulgence. This was during the time when there was the breaking up of the Atlantean land. When there was then waging of the eternal Laws of One with those that worshipped Belial—and those that worshipped the satisfying of physical desire—those that worshipped ease and pleasure in a material world." (640-1; Aug. 22, 1934)

"in Atlantis during period of second upheaval when Sons of Belial and Sons of Law of One made those great changes in the application of the Law of One to material benefits or for the special privileged." (3654-1; Jan. 22, 1944)

This second period of destruction did not entirely destroy Atlantis, according to the Edgar Cayce readings. The land was split into islands. Some lost their lives and some migrated elsewhere, but many stayed and for a while things quieted down. A high state of civilization continued, for electricity is mentioned and atomic energy implied.

This may have been the period of polar shifting, for climatic changes from temporate to torrid are suggested by "the shifting of the activities of the earth itself."

"in that land now known as the Atlantean during those days when there were the attempts of those to bring quiet, to bring order out of the chaos by the destructive forces that had made for the eruptions in the land, that had divided the lands and had changed not only the temperate to a more torrid region but by the shifting of the activities of the earth itself—that had made the records of those things whereby there might be the cleansing of the body from the pollutions of the world or of the animal kingdom." (884-1; April 9, 1935)

Other readings given years apart surely refer to the same era. Scientific advancement is indicated by allusions to "electrical forces" and radioactive rays are implied. Also the "things" are again mentioned.

"in Atlantean land when there were the attempts to reconstruct the activities of the people after the second of upheavals or breaking up, of the land or continent —applied materially electricity or electrical forces." (1861-2; Nov. 23, 1939)

"in Atlantis during time of readjustment from period of second destruction." (5096-1; April 18, 1944)

"in Atlantean land just after second breaking up of the land owing to misapplication of divine laws upon those things of nature or of the earth; when there were the eruptions from the second using of those influences that were for man's own development, yet becoming destructive forces to flesh when misapplied." (1298-1; Nov. 27, 1936)

"in Atlantis during those periods between the second and last upheaval when there was great antagonism between the Sons of Belial and the Sons of the Law of One—a priestess to the laboring ones, made overtures to the peoples for the acknowledging of the laborers and to make their experience easier—those laborers were considered by many as 'things' rather than individual souls." (1744-1; Nov. 12, 1938)

This last quotation brings us to the end of Atlantean civilization and to the final destruction of the remaining islands of a once great continent.

This, I believe, is the destruction alluded to by Plato. Here the remnant of a once vast civilization, still capable of scientific achievement, is plagued by the problems of selfishness and man's inhumanity to man, problems that beset it from the beginning. In fact, the problems man faces today seem to differ little from those he faced when first he entered materiality.

CHAPTER 5

The Final Destruction

A great many of the life readings deal with this period of time—the final destruction of Atlantis and parallel activity in Egypt. In fact, about fifty percent of all the life readings mentioning Atlantis are concerned with this era. There are several reasons. Probably most important is that Edgar Cayce, according to his own life readings, had an incarnation in Egypt at this time.

Many persons closely associated with Edgar Cayce also had life readings, and these people too had Egyptian incarnations then. This Egyptian period of association was influencing their present lives. Consider the following:

> Q.6: *"Have I known any of the people in a former life with whom I have come in contact in this life?"*
> A.6: *"Most* [of those] *we meet. We meet few people by chance but all are opportunities in one experience or another. We are due them or they are due us certain considerations."* (3246-1)

Thus, according to the Edgar Cayce readings, it is likely rather than unlikely that we have known in past lives most of the people with whom we associate in the present life.

Many of the life readings, although they mention Atlantis, are concerned with happenings in Egypt having to do with Atlanteans who migrated there during the final destruction of the remaining islands. The few quotes I have selected from the many life readings involving Egyptian pre-history indicate the time of the final Atlantean disaster and the fact that, as in the past, the Atlanteans went to various other countries to the east and to the west. The time of these events is so remote (over 10,000 years ago) that few records remain. Those that do are either undiscovered or unrecognized.

Some of the life readings, such as the following, simply mention the third or final destruction:

". . . in the Atlantean land before the third destruction—assisted Alta, the scribe, in preparing a history of the land." (339-1; May 27, 1933)

Others are more specific and mention dates and places to which some of the inhabitants fled to avoid the imminent disaster.

". . . in Atlantis during periods of the breaking up of the land. Set sail for Egypt, but ended up in the Pyrenees in what are now Portuguese, French and Spanish lands. In Calais may still be seen the marks in the chalk cliffs of the entity's followers as attempts [were made] to create a temple activity for the followers of the Law of One. First to establish a library of knowledge in 10,300 B.C. in what later became Alexandria in Egypt." (315-4; June 13, 1934)

The above gives a specific date and also mentions "marks in the chalk cliffs at Calais" which exist today (or which did exist in June 1934, when the reading was given).

The final exodus from Atlantis seems to have been organized. It took place over a longer period of time than Plato indicated. This is illustrated by these two extracts from life readings given about three years apart:

"With the realization of the children of the Law of One that there was to be the final breaking up of the Poseidian-Atlantean lands, there were the emigrations with many of the leaders to the various lands." (1007-3; June 26, 1938)

". . . in the Atlantean land when there was the breaking up of the isles and it had been given out that those that would or were to be saved must journey to the various centers to which the leaders had been given the passports. [The entity was] among those that came first to what is now the Pyrenees and later to the activities, after they had been set up years before, in the Egyptian land." (633-2; July 26, 1935)

Not all of the Atlanteans came east to Europe and Africa. Many, according to the life readings, traveled west to the Americas.

This is deduced from two readings given five years apart. Both refer to migrations westward to escape the *final* destruction of Atlantis.

"in the Atlantean land during those periods when there were the activities that brought about the last destruction through the warring of Sons of Law of One and Sons of Belial—among those sent to what later became the Yucatan land of the Mayan experiences." (1599-1; May 28, 1938)

"in Atlantean land when there were those periods of the last upheavals or the disappearance of the isles of Posedia. [The entity was] among those who went to what later became known as the Inca land—the Peruvian land as called in the present." (3611-1; Dec. 31, 1943)

In the following excerpts are hints that some record of these migrations may be discovered:

"in Atlantis when there was the breaking up of the land, came to what was called the Mayan land or what is now Yucatan—entity was the first to cross the water in the plane or air machine of that period." (1710-3; April 12, 1939)

"in land now known as Yucatan, when there were establishments from Atlantean land—entity in temple as

110

a recorder—were periods of dissension with those in authority; when there were the decisions of most of the people to join with the movement to what is now portions of Arizona—entity chose to remain—records may eventually be discovered again." (5245-1; June 3, 1944)

"in Atlantean land during period of egress before final destruction—coordinated departure activities—journeyed to Central America where some of the temples are being uncovered today [1935]—began practice of cremation, ashes may be found in one of temples prepared for same." (914-1; May 1, 1935)

At the time of these life readings, it was believed that man had been in North and South America for only a few thousand years. This last reading was given in 1935. On February 10, 1935, the Washington *Herald* carried a full-page article about the recent discoveries of F.A. Mitchell Hedges. Mitchell-Hedges, a noted British explorer, and a member of the Maya Committee of the British Museum, had found traces of a civilization on islands off the coast of Central America. This civilization, he stated, "may be a remnant of the fabled Atlantis." The British Museum avoided any reference to Atlantis, but officially stated that "this is an early culture from which the early forms of culture were diffused over Central America." The Museum of the American Indian, Heye Foundation, New York, concurred with the findings of the British Museum according to the newspaper article and wrote Mitchell-Hedges:

"Your own observations and the U.S. Government surveys in Nicaragua prove conclusively that at some remote period a tremendous earth movement of cataclysmic force must have taken place in that part of the world —and your excavations have actually unearthed the cultural artifacts of a prehistoric people that existed prior to that earth movement—your discoveries open up an entirely new vista in regard to the ancient civilizations of the American continent."

On October 4, 1959, the *New York Herald Tribune* carried an article about the discovery of archeological sites in Colombia in the Andes. These sites, characterized by unusual statues, are described as "an archeological mystery for which no definite chronological or cultural links to other known civilizations have been established."

The *San Jose News* of February 13, 1964, carried an article describing finds in the Teohuacan Valley 150 miles south of Mexico City. Several different phases of inhabitation were uncovered. Radiocarbon dates of 7200 B.C. for the early periods were established but Dr. MacNeish, archeologist for the Robert S. Peabody Foundation, stated that the first occupants may have been in the area three or four thousand years earlier—that is, 10,000 to 11,000 years B.C.

A discussion of ancient civilizations in the Americas is to be found in a four-column article in the *New York Times*, December 3, 1961. W. P. Luce describes a modern air tour of Mexico's ancient ruins, and gives details of an archeological site thirty-two miles from Mexico City, so old that even the Aztecs knew nothing about its origin. This is Teotihuacan, the site of the Pyramid of the Sun. The pyramid and its surrounding buildings were ruins hundreds of years before the arrival of Cortez. The pyramid itself has been reconstructed into a structure as tall as a twenty-story skyscraper. From the top one may view a beautiful valley filled with the remains of the once-great Teotihuacan culture. These people were excellent sculptors and painters as well as architects and engineers. Luce says the sculptured representations of the feathered serpent are fashioned with as much talent as the gargoyles on Notre Dame in Paris. The arrangements of the citadel and flanking buildings show a good sense of proportion. However, these ruins raise more questions than they answer. No one knows who built them or why or what happened to the builders.

The following reading sheds some light on the ancestors of the Maya, Inca, Aztec and other old civilizations of Central and South America. It indicates that many different influences have injected themselves into this area, some from Atlantis, some from the Pacific region, and thousands of years later a Mosaic influence. The mound builders of early America apparently came up from Central America.

HLC: *"You will give an historical treatise on the origin and development of the Mayan civilization, answering questions."*

Mr. C: *"Yes. In giving a record of the civilization in this particular portion of the world, it should be remembered that more than one has been and will be found as research progresses. That which we find would be of particular interest would be that which superseded the Aztec civilization, that was so ruthlessly destroyed or interrupted by Cortez.*

"In that preceding this we had rather a combination of sources, or a high civilization that was influenced by injection of forces from other channels, other sources, as will be seen, or may be determined by that which may be given.

"From time as counted in the present we would turn back to 10,600 years before the Prince of Peace came into the land of promise, and find a civilization being disturbed by corruption from within to such measures that the elements join in bringing devastation to a stiff-necked and adulterous people.

"With the second and third upheavals in Atlantis, there were individuals who left those lands and came to this particular portion then visible.

"But, understand, the surface was quite different from that which would be viewed in the present. For rather than being a tropical area, it was more of the temperate, and quite varied in the conditions and positions of the face of the areas themselves.

113

"In following such a civilization as a historical presentation, it may be better understood by taking into consideration the activities of an individual or group—or their contribution to such a civilization. This of necessity, then, would not make for a complete historical fact, but rather the activities of an individual and the followers, or those that chose one of their own as leader.

"Then, with the leavings of the civilization in Atlantis (in Poseidia, more specific), Iltar—with a group of followers that had been of the household of Atlan, the followers of the worship of the ONE—with some ten individuals—left this land Poseidia, and came westward, entering what would now be a portion of Yucatan. And there began, with the activities of the peoples there, the development into a civilization that rose much in the same manner as that which had been in the Atlantean land. Others had left the land later. Others had left earlier. There had been the upheavals also from the land of Mu, or Lemuria, and these had their part in the changing or there was the injection of their tenets in the varied portions of the land, which was much greater in extent until the final upheaval of Atlantis, or the islands that were later upheaved, when much of the contour of the land in Central America and Mexico was changed to that similar in outline to that which may be seen in the present.

"The first temples that were erected by Iltar and his followers were destroyed at the period of change physically in the contours of the land. That now being found, and a portion already discovered that has lain in waste for many centuries, was then a combination of those peoples from Mu, Oz, and Atlantis." (5750-1; Nov. 12, 1933)

As I understand the preceding, man had migrated to South and Central America and to the western part of North America from Atlantis and from lands in the Pacific

Ocean. This had taken place from 28,000 B.C. (the time of the second upheavals in Atlantis) to around 10,000 B.C. (the time of the final destruction of Atlantis). During the final destruction, some of the settled portions of Central and South America sank and the Caribbean area assumed its present land contours.

The inhabitants of Central and South America were now a mixture of those who had come earlier from Atlantis and the Pacific area and those who had come at the final destruction of Atlantis, as indicated by the following paragraph from the same reading (5750-1).

"Hence, these places partook of the earlier portions of that peoples called the Incal; though the Incals were themselves the successors of those of Oz, or Og, in the Peruvian land, and Mu in the southern portions of that now called California and Mexico and southern New Mexico in the United States."

This was not the end of migrations to the Americas, though, for the same reading continues with a statement suggesting a Mosaic influx.

"This again found a change when there were the injections from those peoples that came with the division of the peoples in that called the promised land. Hence we may find in these ruins that which partakes of the Egyptian, Lemurian and Oz civilizations, and the later activities partaking even of the Mosaic activities." (5750-1)

The reading then discusses the type of ruins characteristic of each period. Some circular stones, used in connection with religious ceremonies, are said to date back to early descendants of the Atlanteans.

The pyramids and altars before the doors of temples were associated with other groups. Much later there was supposedly a Jewish or Mosaic influence.

The intermingling of various groups resulted in a mixed civilization which developed in Yucatan and Mexico near

115

where Mexico City stands today. Some of these people migrated to the southwestern United States. Others later moved into the central and eastern portions of America and became what is referred to as the Mound Builders.

Some corroboration of these statements from Edgar Cayce's life reading may be found in the *Encyclopaedia Britannica* (Vol. 12, 1954) in the section "Indians of North America." In a discussion of the Indians in various parts of the United States there is the statement, "The American Indian appears not to represent a homogeneous racial stock, though it has been customary so to describe him. . . . It is likely that the peopling of the American continents was accomplished over a long period of time, in successive waves of migration. Moreover, these succeeding waves were doubtless composed of people of different points of origin, quite likely of different language stock, and certainly of nonhomogeneous physical types." Turning again to. the *Book of the Hopi* by Frank Waters, the destruction of the third world sounds very much like the final destruction of Atlantis. Hopi myth and legend describe this third world as one of a rapidly increasing population, in which great cities were created and crafts flourished. One tribe made a "patuwvota" (shield of hide) which could fly through the air with people on it and this was used in warfare. The people became so corrupt, wicked and warlike that their world was destroyed, this time by a great flood. "Waves higher than mountains rolled in on the land and continents broke asunder and sank beneath the seas." Some were saved by traveling in boats from island to island until they reached a great land. The Hopi legends continue with the migrations of various clans. There are indications in symbols and stories which have been handed down that the ancestors of the Hopi were related to the Mound Builders and that various clans and tribes migrated to the southwestern United States from a land to the south. The legendary history in this *Book of the Hopi,* first published in 1963, agrees uncannily with

116

material given in life readings twenty to thirty years previously.

Volume 15 of the Encyclopaedia Britannica describes the Mound Builders as being prehistoric inhabitants of America. Some of their mounds are quite impressive in size. One in Ohio, representing a serpent, is 1348 feet long. The jaws of the snake are seventy-five feet across; the body is thirty feet wide and five feet high. Other mounds in Wisconsin are gigantic earthen figures of birds, mammals and reptiles. The purpose of the mounds is not known— they are supposed to be totemic. Other type mounds are found in Tennessee along with graves. A study of the skulls from the mounds proves these Stone Age men were not all of one race.

This reading (5750-1) concerning the early inhabitants of America raises as many questions as it answers, but recent discoveries are pushing back the age of man in the Americas and uncovering evidence for pre-Columbian communication between the hemispheres.

To those who have studied the data in the A.R.E. files it is no longer surprising that recent research keeps turning up evidence for ancient peoples in the areas designated by Edgar Cayce in life readings given over thirty years ago.

In the April 28th, 1967, issue of *The New York Times,* there is an article about finds of American and Mexican archeologists at Puebla, a town about one hundred miles southeast of Mexico City. Stone tools, "generally unlike any other known New World artifacts," were discovered in an old river bed. Also found in the same strata were remains of Ice Age animals such as antelope, wolf, horses, camels and sloths. Overlaying the tools and bones was a layer of ash from Ixtacihuall, a famous Mexican volcano. Carbon 14 tests by the U.S. Geological Survey of a tree burned in the ash fall dates the fall at more than 40,000 years ago. Snail and clam shells in a nearby strata, thought to be about the same age as the bones and tools, were dated at more than 35,000 years old.

The *Times* reporter who interviewed one of the archeologists by phone quotes her as saying, "We have no hints of the type of peoples who might have inhabited the area."

This same reading (5750-1) closes on a note of prophecy in answer to a question:

> Q.4: *"In which pyramid or temple are the records mentioned in the readings given through this channel on Atlantis, in April, 1932?"* (This refers to the 364 series of readings.)
> A.4: *"As given, that temple was destroyed at the time there was the last destruction in Atlantis.*
>
> *"Yet, as the time draws nigh when the changes are to come about, there may be the opening of those three places where the records are one, to those that are the initiates in the knowledge of the One God:*
>
> *"The temple by Iltar will then rise again. Also there will be the opening of the temple or hall of records in Egypt, and those records that were put into the heart of the Atlantean land may also be found there—that have been kept, for those that are of that group. The records are One."* (5750-1; Nov. 12, 1933)

The discovery of any sort of records pertaining to Atlantis, besides causing an uproar in the archeological field, should offer conclusive validation of Edgar Cayce's Atlantean life readings.

Some Atlanteans came directly to Egypt. But others went first to what is now Spain or Portugal, particularly the Pyrenees region. This fact is mentioned in readings given ten years apart.

> *"in Atlantean land when there was knowledge that there soon was to be the destruction of that land and there were attempts of individuals to leave the land. Entity among those who went to Egypt."* (708-1; Oct. 25, 1934)
> *"among Atlanteans who first came to Egypt, journeyed to what is now a portion of Portugal or the Pyrenees*

where some Atlaneans had set up temple activity, aided in decorations of temple." (1123-1; Feb. 19, 1936)

"in Atlantis when there was the breaking up of the land—among those that went to what is now the Spanish land; while many changed to the Egyptian land the entity remained in Pyrenees and established those tenets and truths that aided much until hordes from the African land brought destruction to those people." (3541-1; Jan. 10, 1944)

"in Atlantis at time of disputes when many sent to many lands, [the entity] a mathematician, came to Pyrenees, journeyed through the air, later came to Egypt." (This reading mentions later that this person became famous as a builder of dams and buildings. 2677-1; Jan. 27, 1942)

The final destruction of Atlantis, or the remaining islands, may have been sudden and violent, but evidently the people had warnings of what might happen. Individual references in the Edgar Cayce life readings indicate an organized exodus. The survivors attempted to continue their way of life in their new homes, as we can see by the various occupations listed in readings referring to this period.

"conducted people from Atlantis to Egypt previous to last destruction—worked with adorning buildings with gems and precious stones." (955-1; July 20, 1935)

"among those who came from Atlantis, [to Egypt], in command of the fleets or ships, explored along waterways." (797-1)

"among those who journeyed from Atlantean land to Egypt, entity young at time, aided in development of mechanical appliances for cutting stone, etc." (1177-1)

"came to Egypt from Pyrenees land, hence came with latter portion of those from Atlantean land." (1458-1)

"in Egyptian land when there was the entering of those that sought aid or refuge from turmoil arising in native

119

land. *The entity among those that came from Atlantean land and aided in replenishing and rebuilding of the temple service, for entity was of household that followed Law of One."* (439-1; Nov. 13, 1933)

"in Atlantean land when divisions arose with destruction coming upon the land, chose to go with groups going to Egypt, what would be known as a chemist, aided in making lands of the Nile more productive." (1842-1; March 14, 1939)

In order to understand the extracts concerning this era, we should know something of what was happening in Egypt at this time. Judging from material gathered from a number of individual and general life readings covering this period, it seems that from between 10,000 and 11,000 B.C. a tribe from the Carpathian region invaded and conquered Egypt. One of the leaders of this tribe was a priest named Ra-Ta. Ra-Ta was Edgar Cayce (or Edgar Cayce was Ra-Ta, depending upon your point of view). In Egypt Ra-Ta's religious teachings attracted a large following. However, there was already political friction in Egypt and tension between the ruling classes and the native Egyptians. Ra-Ta was caught up in this political intrigue, and after a native rebellion, he was banished for nine years to what is now Abyssinia.

At the height of the confusion refugees began arriving in Egypt from Atlantis. The Atlanteans, scientifically more advanced than the Egyptians, found little in common with the inhabitants of Egypt, and began to set up their old way of life. Leaders of the ruling class and leaders of the native rebellion soon realized that these incoming Atlanteans with their superior scientific knowledge and radically different social and religious views posed a new threat. A leader had to be found, around whom the people could rally, to turn the power of the Atlanteans into constructive channels. In an effort to bring some order out of the chaos the leaders in power decided to recall the priest from banishment. Only he might correlate the activities of all these conflicting groups. This move was successful and with the cooperation of the rulers of Egypt, the priest, the Atlanteans and the natives there ensued a period of great advancement in human relations. The then civilized portions of the world enjoyed a period of moral, mental, spiritual and physical development.

Combination hospital and educational institutions (called the Temple of Sacrifice and the Temple of Beauty) were set up, and probably functioned like the psychiatric wing of a modern hospital. There the masses flocked for mental as well as physical therapy. Evidently, besides low mental development and/or lack of moral judgment and self-control, some people classed as servants or "things" or "automatons" had physical deformities linking them to the animal world. They may have had tails, feathers, or scales. This was a holdover from the early projection of souls into materiality for selfish purposes at which time monstrosities as well as creatures of beauty were created. It seems that these institutions of physical and psychic healing were successful; in fact, there was a worldwide dissemination of ideas, knowledge and teachings. The few dates given concerning this period indicate that all this took place 10,000 to 11,000 years B.C.

Information on this period was collected from life readings of both Atlantean and early Egyptian incarnations under the headings Migrations to Egypt, Recall of the Priest, Correlation of Activities, Temple Beautiful and Temple of Sacrifice, Records and Dates. A great number of quotations from individual life readings, many given years apart, lend these events an aura of reality. I cannot, at this time, "prove" this material is history, not fiction. But I don't think anyone can disprove it. And Edgar Cayce insists that records *exist* of the Atlantean civilization. Since he has been accurate in the past, I should not be surprised if some day these records are discovered.

Let us look at the collection of readings mentioning migrations to the Pyrenees and to Egypt.

"in Egypt but of the Atlantean people when there was the exodus to what is now the Spanish or Pyrenees land, and then to Egypt. With the establishing of the coalition between Egyptians and Atlanteans aided in preparations for vocational guidance, for various groups." (2916-1; Feb. 11, 1943)

"in Spanish land when there were those who were interpreters of the seal through which elements were used for heat, power, electrical forces. Thus none of the modern conveniences are a mystery at all, even though they may not be understood; for entity has expected to see same again." (3574-2; Jan. 20, 1944)

"in Egypt when there were gatherings of those that had escaped from the land that was destroyed or the Atlantean land. Entity persuaded many to make for activities that would preserve to the people what would be recipes, placards, drawings, etc. These were first of such to be brought to Egyptian natives and first attempts to make for a written language." (516-2; Feb. 24, 1934)

Various occupations were mentioned indicating an advanced civilization.

"came into Egypt from Atlantis when very young in years, became what today would be an instructor in psychological tests." (1751-1; Nov. 18, 1938)

"an Atlantean who came to Egypt, aided in styling for dress and conveniences for home." (1120-1; Feb. 13, 1936)

There is an indication that many of the native Egyptians of that period were deficient physically, mentally or morally.

"in Egyptian land when there were those people from Atlantis who had come into the land—the third Atlantean child born in Egypt—to many of the natives, to

122

many who followed the teachings of Ra-Ta it was a curiosity for it was perfect in body, in form and in color." (3645-1; Jan. 15, 1944)

"came into Egypt when the children of the Law of One realized there was to be the breaking up of the Poseidian or Atlantean land." This reading mentions attempts to coordinate teachings with priest of that period, mentions establishment of Temple of Sacrifice and Temple Beautiful—*"these offered a channel for purging body and mind as a school or hospital would today."* (1007-3; June 26, 1938)

"among Atlanteans who came into Egypt during time of return of priest and the establishment of penal law as well as moral and spiritual law." (1007-1; Sept. 20, 1935)

The following extracts refer to the banishment and recall of the priest. Note the consistency of statements made in life readings for separate individuals, readings which were given over a period of five years.

"in Egypt, one of the guards sent with priest to what is now Abyssinian land during nine years of priest's banishment." (1650-1; July 29, 1938)

"in Egypt during turmoils, banishment of priest and gatherings from Atlantean land—came from Parthenian or Persian lands from which the conquerors then of Egypt had come." (1472-1; Nov. 6, 1937)

"in Egypt, gave first consideration for unifying the land by return of priest and the acceptance of activities of those from Atlantean land." (1767-2; Jan 8, 1939)

"in Egypt when there were attempts to induce the king to recall the priest—aided in correlating with Atlanteans and general populace the reasons for recall of priest." (2834-1; Oct. 27, 1942)

The following extract, given for a prayer group (some of

whom were associated with Edgar Cayce in Egypt), gives more details of 'the recall of the priest and activities in Egypt during that period.

> "When the Atlanteans in that experience began to influence the spiritual and moral life of the Egyptians, during those turmoils which had arisen through the Rebellions as indicated, there came that desire, that purpose—especially on the part of the natives, as well as those who had been adherents partly to the tenets of the priest—that the priest be returned, that there might be a better understanding. For the native leaders, especially, realized that their own activities or representation in the spiritual, moral and religious life would be destroyed if there was the adhering to the tenets being presented by the Atlanteans.
>
> "And, as might be termed in the present, some indicated that the priest alone would be a match for those activities of some of the stronger or more forward Atlanteans. For they had brought with them (as had the priest) many things, or individuals, or entities, that were without purpose, or merely automatons, to labor or act for the leaders in the various spheres of activity.*
>
> "And, as the natives found, such beings were being classified or judged to be such as many of the natives of the land. Hence there were overtures made to the ruler, and to those in authority with same, that the priest be recalled.
>
> "With the return of the priest there began the choosing as to who was to be considered in authority, in the spiritual precepts. And there was the activity of the priest in choosing entities, individuals from all walks of life, all stations—whether in authority in the political or

---

* Evidently even at this relatively late date there were still in existence a number of creatures used as slaves. These beings were discussed in previous chapters.

the economic, or the general affairs of the land." (281-43)

The wisdom of the Egyptians in recalling the priest was soon justified. Not only did the political tension relax, but the priest began establishing institutions for the hospitalization and education of the "things"—the beings who were used as slaves.

"Thus, as has been indicated, there arose the needs for the Temple of Sacrifice, where entities, individuals, might offer themselves for the purification of their bodies, that they first might be channels through which there might come entities, souls, manifesting in the earth with the entire activity of body, mind and soul. It was the same intent as had been the purpose of the priest, in the choice of that individual through whom the pure race, the pure activities of a better purpose might be made manifest.

"This, to be sure, caused a great deal of discussion, dissension, among the leaders in those groups of the Atlanteans. Thus, as has been indicated, there were the needs for the priest to enter into that period of medication, of setting himself aside, purifying self through continuous prayer, continuous seeking, continuous opening of those forces.

"Thus we had the priest's rejuvenation, or the turning back of age as it were, or those conditions which would hinder the activities. And this began that period in which even members of the present Prayer Group prayed and meditated with the entity; not in companionship, to be sure, but in their OWN desire that there might be a unifying of the purposes, the desires." (281-43)

The reading goes on to describe the Temple Beautiful and Temple of Sacrifice by

"comparing same to the present hospitals where there might be operative measures used for the removal of

125

such things as tumors, breaks, growths or the like.
"The Temple of Sacrifice was a physical experience, while the Temple Beautiful was rather of the mental, in which there was the spiritualization—not idolizing, but crystallizing of activities or services to a special purpose—or specializing in preparation for given officers of activity." (281-43; Nov. 1, 1939)

The following extracts refer to the recall of the priest and also hint at the type of activity associated with his recall. Whether the readings were given seven days apart or six years apart, they are consistent in their description of the activities taking place in Egypt and Atlantis at this period.

"made trips to and from Poseidian or Atlantean land during times of turmoils when many individuals and groups went to and from Atlantis—settled in Egypt after restoration of priest Ra-Ta." (423-3; Jan. 22, 1934)
"priestess in temple in Atlantis, when there was the breaking up of peoples owing to destructive forces went into Egypt, aided in recall of priest." (1042-2; April 11, 1936)

All of these extracts from different individual life readings refer to the Egyptian priest specifically.

"in Atlantis when there was rebellions by children of Belial and preparations for leaving because of upheavals and influences that were to bring about the complete destruction—journeyed to what is now a part of Spain, later to the Egyptian land, with recall of priest aided in correlation of activities." (2283-1; June 14, 1940)
"in Egypt during period of reconstruction when priest returned for bringing order out of chaos, by rebellions of natives as well as theological activities of Atlanteans. Entity active in aiding individuals not only to become

126

better channels for propagation of families but in vocational guidance." (2272-1; June 7, 1940)

The next four extracts are most specific regarding activities in the temples.

"in Egypt in periods of rebellion [mentions banishment of priest, advent of Atlanteans and recall of priest and reconciliations] *entity active in hospitalization for variations in physical or physiognomy of race."* (2940-1; March 21, 1943)

"in Egypt—active in clarifying how there might be political, material, spiritual progress through recall of priest." (2946-2; May 16, 1943)

"in Egyptian land during those periods of reconstruction; for the entity was among the Atlanteans who came into the land—though not outwardly active in the disputes that arose. With the re-establishing of the priest and the variations wrought by the reconstruction in the various temples or the various means for changing the characteristics of groups and individuals the entity was among those who interpreted the same in the music of the temple worship or temple service." (2421-2; Feb. 7, 1941)

"in Egypt, a native of the lands to which the priest was banished, returned with the priest—attempted to make song and dance a part of Temple service—first to combine reeds and lyre or the stringed instruments as a combination for the songs of the Atlanteans the natives's chant, the wild revelry of its own land, to arouse the emotions necessary for concerted activity of the peoples." (1476-1; Nov. 14, 1937)

Although the scientific development at this time does not seem to have been as great as at the time of the second destruction and during the period between second and final destruction, there still was some degree of technology remaining.

127

*"in Atlantean land when there was the breaking up of
the land owing to the attempts of the Sons of Belial to
use the activities of the Sons of the Law of One for self-
indulgence, self-aggrandizement because of desires for
activities in which the baser metals, the baser activities
might be turned into use for pleasures of the Sons of
Belial; used such gases, liquid air, explosives, things
having to do with both creative and destructive forces—
entity studied these, and these activities, with those with
whom entity journeyed to the Egyptian land. Brought
both good and bad in the Egyptian land—some of
natives and some who rebelled against the king attempted to use these (though not part of this entity's
experience). Entity's knowledge of same brought disturbing forces; with return of priest these turned into
constructive channels, as in hospitalization, manners of
moving great stone figures, etc."* (2147-1; March 16,
1940)

*"in Egypt, of native people, became active with return of
priest as interpreter of speech of Atlantean land and
Gobi land."* (1487-1; Nov. 28, 1937)

*"of Atlantean people but born in Egypt in period of
rebuilding after turmoils—aided others to become emissaries, going itself to Gobi land."* (3420-1; Dec. 17,
1943)

Before I quote further from readings that deal with
world travel, let us consider some that mention the Temple
of Beauty specifically and the activities associated with
these hospital-like institutions. Even though these temples
were in Egypt a number of Atlanteans were associated with
their construction and use:

*"in Atlantean land when there was the breaking up of
the land through use of spiritual truths for material gains
of physical power. Administered in Temple of Sun from
which all power was used for aid in material things—
aided in giving instruction for preservation of lives to go*

128

to other lands—entity came to Egypt and in later years saw in Temple of Sacrifice and Temple of Beauty or Temple Beautiful the perfection and preservation of bodies of even those the entity and associates had considered rabble—saw that the Lord is not a respecter of persons but loves those that love their brethren." (1152-1; April 20, 1936)

"came from Atlantis into Egypt when young in years. Became supervisor over graineries, storehouses of gold and precious stones, the divisions of these things that were to go to those in positions of authority for the sustaining of the land and for propagation of knowledge as might be of a helpful nature. Entity in position of engineer in broader sense not only in being able to lay out lands, and construction of bridges, viaducts, ships etc., but in holy things—in building altars in Temple Beautiful and Temple of Sacrifice." (1574-1; April 19, 1938)

The following extract indicates that there had been temples in Atlantis similar to the ones constructed in Egypt.

"of Atlanteans who came into Egypt, interpreted in Temple Beautiful those beauties of temples in Poseidia." (1193-1; April 30, 1936)

The next group of extracts indicates some of the uses or accomplishments of these temples.

"in Egypt during times of turmoils when there were sojourners from Atlantis. As a teacher, organized groups of those purified in Temple of Sacrifice for specific purposes—artisans, agriculturalists, etc." (1082-3; Nov. 12, 1937)

"in Egyptian land during periods of rebuilding of material, religious and social order, reared with children of young king, became favorite of king in activities in

*which there were the classifying of groups of individuals
for their special service in the various formations and
activities, in the commercial sense as well as in the
building of relationships that had to do with the Temple
Beautiful and Temple of Sacrifice; these temples were on
the order of what today we call our educational
institutions and hospitals that prepared men and women
of that period for greater service to their country and to
their people for glory of creative forces or God."*
(2524-1; July 2, 1941)

*"Hence we find the entity was active especially in the
influences for the establishing of the Temples of
Sacrifice, and the Temple Beautiful; that represented or
offered a channel through which there was a purging of
the bodies as well as the minds, in the manners as we
have indicated. It was much in the same way and
manner that our hospital institutions and educational
institutions of today would purge the individual from
disease that wrecks body and mind; as well as the
preparation of the individual through the educational
forces for the perpetuation of the good or the best in the
race."* (1007-3; June 26, 1938)

Although these readings were given years apart, the
following extracts are grouped together because they all
mention physical changes that were accomplished in the
Egyptian temples:

*"in Atlantis when young and old were being sent to
other lands—brought with others understanding to those
in Egyptian land as to the activities in which there might
be (and became later) a unifying of purpose in the
teachings of the priest in that experience as to how
through the activities of the Temple of Sacrifice as well
as the Temple Beautiful, bodies as well as minds were
prepared for the special service in given directions in
their relationships with the material, the mental, the
spiritual affairs of men."* (1641-1; July 17, 1938)

130

"in Atlantean land when groups were being sent to other lands for various purpose—among those coming to Egypt. With establishing of Temple of Sacrifice entity set about to use truths and tenets that had been part of Atlantean experience, these used as suggestions with elements and drugs used as sedatives for activities in Temple of Sacrifice, or for surgery, in preparing individuals for definite services by removal of those things that would cause one to become different-minded because of the relationships to the activities in a pre-existence or pre-period of materiality." (5118-1; April 19, 1944)

This extract and the following one suggest that particular physical characteristics in one life may result from activities in a previous one.

"in Egypt when individuals sought to prepare themselves for service to fellowmen as a whole. Aided in Temple of Sacrifice for cleansing of body of many from appendages that hindered or took hold upon those things that had been a part of the old disturbances among men—helped in regeneration of people through tenets of priest and Atlanteans." (1837-1; March 4, 1939)

Evidently it was possible to produce radical physical changes in the initiates in these temples, and some of these changes in individuals were to have an influence on future generations:

"in Egypt during correlation of activities of natives, priest and Atlanteans—entity part Egyptian, part Atlantean—associated with activities when there was the preparing and presenting of ways and manners in which the race might be changed." (1695-1; Sept. 29, 1938)

"in Egypt during period of restoring of order with return of priest—born of those people of purer race for definite

activities in Temple Beautiful and Temple of Sacrifice."
(1709-3; Nov. 11, 1939)

The next reading also refers to the institutions in Egypt
where mental and physical changes were effected.

*"in Egypt at time of turmoils and strife between natives,
household of king and those entering from Atlantean
land—later with reestablishment of priest aided in
Temple Beautiful and Temple of Sacrifice in hospitalization and interpretations of those things in their
mental relationships to those that had through sacrifice rid themselves of those things that were still as appendages, still these materializations of matter as
associated with the physical body."* (1404-1; July 5,
1937)

This period must have been one of great progress and
one filled with hope and joy for the "things" or slaves. The
scientific knowledge of the Atlanteans was turned to
constructive purposes and applied in these Egyptian
temples, enabling the slaves or "things" to rid themselves
of mental and physical hindrances to their development.

*"in Egypt during period of reconstruction, active in
Temple of Sacrifice, active in using those things presented by Atlanteans where electrical forces, as termed
in the present, were used as means for removal of
forms of appendages and those things that caused
reactions in the brain forces of the body."* (2927-1;
March 1, 1943)
*"an Atlantean who came to Egypt—helped some of
people to throw off the appendages or hindrances of the
animal forces, aided many people of many tongues and
many lands, aided preparation for those going into
Temple of Sacrifice and Temple Beautiful."* (774-4;
March 30, 1936)

Not only were the individuals who went through these Temples changed, but their children were also:

> *"in Egypt—offspring of those who had entered Temple of Sacrifice—chosen by priest as well as by king's followers and followers of Atlanteans—entity an example of what might be outcome of such preparations before period of conception."* (2144-1; March 11, 1940)

The preceding extracts may sound fantastic but no more so than the headlines of November 20, 1966. *The Virginian Pilot,* in its "Lighthouse" section, carried a full-page article about experiments being conducted on the human brain with electricity and chemicals. The subtitle of the article asks, "Is Mind Control the Next Step in Human Evolution?" The article describes how enraged animals were suddenly rendered tranquil with electrical impulses to the brain. Withdrawn mental patients, with tiny electrical wires inserted into their brains, were made aware of the world; depressed persons had their emotions, impulses and moods changed in a similar manner. Research is proceeding at a pace that will make present brainwashing techniques and effects seem like child's play. The control of the chemical and electrical activity of the brain, the article asserts, offers the possibilities of "overcoming mental illness, retraining damaged minds, helping the retarded to learn, enhancing human intelligence to undreamed of height, and freeing humans from harmful emotions," but it could also "fashion a prison for mankind and standardize behavior to the point of slavery."

These last few sentences from a 1966 newspaper sound almost like the Edgar Cayce readings describing the control of "things" in Atlantis. Any why not? For if reincarnation is a fact, the techniques are simply being *rediscovered* by their originators. The same article quotes Dr. Heath of Tulane University: "With the use of chemical brain-control agents it may be possible to control the individual and the masses and to do this unobtrusively and without the active

133

cooperation of the victims—not a question of the future—it is here."

The following extract sounds as if a similar technique was used in Atlantis:

> *"among those that were set upon to apply their abilities in relationship to the various conditions that were to be brought about to impel a people to submit to the influences that might be brought to bear."* (Additional data in the reading indicate that electrical and mechanical appliances were used to accomplish this. 440-1; Nov. 14, 1933)

Although *The Virginian Pilot* article is a recent one, it is by no means the only one. In October, 1956, the *Cleveland Press* carried an article entitled "Scientist Sees Human Robots with Built-In Brains." Curtiss R. Schafer, a project engineer with Norden-Keyat Corporation, warned that some day tiny radios placed in the brain may make possible the enslavement of entire nations. Such equipment might enable the blind to see by inducing electric currents in the optic nerves. On the other hand, such research might be used to equip a child with a socket mounted under the scalp from which electrodes extended to selected areas of the brain. Later a miniature radio receiver and antenna could be plugged into the socket. Schafer says, "From that time on, the child's sensory perceptions and muscular activity could be either modified or completely controlled by bio-electric signals radiated from state-controlled transmitters. The 'once-human being' would be the cheapest of machines to create and operate." Shades of Atlantis!

Another article in *The Virginian Pilot* (November 27, 1966) describes a technique that approaches even closer to what may have occurred long ago in Atlantis when humans "became entangled in matter." The article "Clones Shadow Human Race" quotes Professor Joshua Lederberg, a Nobel Prize winning geneticist, as saying that it may soon be possible to propagate people the way we propagate roses—

by taking the equivalent of cuttings. This would make it possible to create dozens—or hundreds—of identical individuals. The essential features of the technique have already been demonstrated in frogs and may someday be achieved in higher animals. "The procedure would be to take a nucleus from the cell of an individual it is desired to duplicate and implant it into a human ovary cell which would then be implanted into the womb to develop. The normal fertilized egg contains genetic material from both parents. But the cell nucleus from any tissue in an individual's body contains the complete genetic 'blueprint' belonging to him. Thus, by using this as a 'cutting' from which to propagate a new individual, an identical twin should result." Professor Lederberg says these possibilities raise questions about what we understand as human identity and individuality. "Human 'clones,' as such a propagated strain of genetically identical people would be called, might be able to communicate with exceptional ease, as identical twins can. Organs might be transplanted from one to another without difficulty." However, such clones "would find themselves in an evolutionary rut, suitable for only one specialized role. So clone propagation would have to be supplemented by conventional propagation to maintain genetic variability." Such procedures might be irresistible for breeders of race horses and prize cattle, but, says Lederberg, biological discoveries may lead into still stranger territory. Lederberg sounds like an old Atlantean when he says, "it may become possible to incorporate part of a human nucleus into the germ cell of some animal, say a gorilla, which might produce various 'sub-human' hybrids."

Let us leave these troublesome thoughts, which may be the brain children of reincarnated Atlanteans, and look at the extracts describing the positive efforts of the Atlanteans and the teachings of the Priest Ra-Ta in Egypt.

The following extract mentions Atlanteans coming into Egypt and indicates that good results were obtained from the rehabilitation of individuals in the Egyptian temples.

135

The cooperation of the Egyptians and Atlanteans resulted in benefits to mankind in general.

> *"in Atlantis entity was the one who received the messages as to the needs of the dividing of the Children of the Law of One for the preservation of the truths of same in other lands, among those directors of expeditions to Egypt, Pyrenees, and to Yucatan and land of Og, just before breaking up of the Atlantean land. Later, with the revivifying of the priest in Egypt, the entity [was] among those that set about the unifying of the teachings of the Atlanteans, the Egyptians (as they would be called today) the Indians, the Indo-Chinans, the Mongoloids and the Aryan peoples. All these were activities of the entity, for he was the messenger or message bearer or means through which the transmissions of messages were set up."* (1681-1; Sept. 7, 1938)

The three extracts which follow were given months and years apart, but they probably refer to this same period. They also suggest that world travel is a much older happening than is commonly supposed.

> *"one of Atlanteans that came into Egypt, aided in quelling the people—bringing reason concerted activity among rulers and those in power, politically and religiously not only in Egypt but to many lands to which emissaries were sent."* (445-1; Nov. 16, 1933)

> *"among young Atlanteans brought into Egypt, acted as secretary to priest instructing those going out for service in other lands."* (1872-1; May 5, 1939)

> *"in Atlantean land when there were those activities that changed the dwellings of the peoples, among the younger of those who came in to Egypt"*—mentions united efforts of Atlanteans and Egyptians in establishing hospitalization and medical care—*"entity was what would today be called a psychoanalyst."* (2002-1; Sept. 14, 1939)

Not only Atlanteans came into Egypt at this time:

"a Persian who came into Egypt at time of reconstruction, an instructor or helper of those 'things,' or automatons as would be called today, to a better understanding." (2570-1; Aug. 9, 1941)

The following extracts from Egyptian rather than Atlantean incarnations, mention the rebellion, the reconstruction period and the return of the priest.

"in Egypt during time of rebellion and turmoils between priest and king"—goes on to say that with reetablishment of priest a unity of effort resulted from the combining of the teachings of the Priest Ra-Ta and the teachings of those *"from Atlantis, India, Mongolia, Carpathia."* (991-1; Aug. 16, 1935)
"in Egyptian land (as now called) when there was the reestablishment of the priest as well as analyzing and stabilizing of the tenets from the Atlantean groups and the classifying and dividing of peoples into various services in the activities during that expanding, developing period—among healers or developments in which there was the compounding of elements of mineral kingdom as applied to human ills, disfigurements or disturbances in body." (2077-1; Jan. 15, 1940)

The following extracts indicate the activities of this period—the work with groups of people done in the temples. They emphasize the mental and physical changes wrought upon individuals and groups, changes that not only enabled these people to live a more productive life, but brought them closer to the creative forces or God.

"in Egypt at time of reconstruction [mentions Temple Beautiful and Temple of Sacrifice and entrance of Atlanteans and those from other lands] *a recorder of*

influences that brought physical and mental changes in groups." (2762-1; June 12, 1942)

"in Egypt during time of cooperation between king, priest and Atlanteans—aided in setting up procedures for cleansing and remaking bodies for greater service— entity purified in Temple of Sacrifice—helped establish homes for those thus cleansed." (2154-1; March 23, 1940)

"in Egypt during period of turmoils and strife when those people who had settled in the land attempted to build for the people roundabout an understanding of the relationship of man to fellowman, of man to the creative forces." (1143-2; April 18, 1936)

As the following reading indicates, some of the Atlanteans questioned the activities of this Egyptian priest who was recalled from banishment to a position of leadership and power. But later, when his purposes were understood, they joined in helping him.

"in Egyptian land during those periods of reconstruction when the banishment of the priest was at an end and there were many entering from the Atlantean land. The entity was an Atlantean who questioned the priest—as many of those who were active in that experience—yet later becoming a helper in that needed for the classifying of the activities, both as to the activities of the entity's own people and the Egyptians as well the priest's people who sojourned there." (2031-1; Oct. 21, 1939)

The following extracts have been collected from a number of life readings mentioning Egyptian incarnation. These individuals seem to have lived at this period of reconstruction in Egypt and to have been associated with the priest Ra-Ta or some Atlanteans. Some had Atlantean parents:

"in Egypt at time of reconstruction—among Atlanteans born in that land—when there was the choosing of individuals to fulfill certain stations or places in the distribution of the ideals pertaining to preparation for better living and better facilities—entity attempted to reconstruct for many of those peoples the various manners of conveniences through the use of unseen powers or forces, or the chemical and electrical energies." (2419-1; Dec. 12, 1940)

"in Egypt, among offspring of Atlanteans, worked in hospitals and with ills of body and mind." (2153-3; July 29, 1940)

"of Atlantean people born in Egypt at time of correlating teachings of various lands. Helped establish customs of dress and headwear." (1033-1; Oct. 26, 1935)

Some were of mixed parentage:

"in Egypt keeper of records of schools, recreation halls, preparation of people for their activities whether in mines, fields, art, trade, etc.—this at time when there was the preparation of people to become emisarries, teachers, etc of those things that had been gathered—when there had been the correlating of tenets from various lands—entity was offspring of Atlanteans as associated with natives of the land." (1610-2; June 29, 1938)

Others were Egyptians:

"in Egypt when tempering as it were between King, Priest and people from Atlantean land—active in Temple Beautiful and Temple of Sacrifice—what would be called cartoonist or artist: one who drew those things that might build character, purposes, desires in individual activities of individuals, as well as those things that presented manners for others to follow." (1597-1; April 27, 1938)

"in Egypt—keeper of graineries at time of reestablishment of relations between priest, king, the Atlanteans and people of other lands. Grain was exchanged for perfumes, spices, gold and animals from other lands." (1587-1; May 3, 1938)

"in Egypt at time of settlement of strife through activities of Atlanteans, a historian, a keeper of records for advancement and development." (1731-1; Nov. 3, 1938)

"in Egypt at time of correlation of teachings of Atlanteans and those of other lands—as a counselor distributed knowledge for protection of food, protection from droughts, etc." (1347-1; March 10, 1937)

"in Egypt at time of reconstruction [mentions coalition of priest and Atlanteans] *work then like insurance today."* (3111-2; Oct. 28, 1943)

"in Egypt when people of Atlantean land came in bringing laws for use of forces of nature for man's convenience—associated with activities in which individuals were fitted for special service owing to their individual development—head of department of what you would call education or commerce." (1554-2; March 24, 1938)

The next few suggest that cooperation of various groups in Egypt produced an enlightened people who attempted to spread their knowledge throughout the world. The readings indicate contact and trade with many lands, particularly China, India, and Indo-China.

"in Egyptian land during period of reconstruction when there was a coalition between king, priest and Atlanteans as well as teachings from Gobi and land of Said [probably India]—*aided in preparation of individuals for betterment of race and vocational guidance."* (2280-1; June 15, 1940)

"in Egypt when emissaries sent to other lands because of activities of priests, natives and Atlanteans—entity went

to Golden City, rose to power in land, not Gobi, but nearby in what is now Siam or Indo-China." (2163-1; April 8, 1940)

The next three extracts refer to the dissemination of spiritual teachings and to the development of commerce and trade on a world wide scale.

"in Egypt during up-building of land when natives and Atlanteans were making associations with other nations, not only commercial but mental and spiritual." (1113-1; Feb. 4, 1936)

"in Egypt when there were the reuniting of the efforts of the king, the priest and those people from the Atlantean land to become a commercial as well as a religious influence in affairs of known world—entity among natives raised to power by the king. Aided in advancing commercial activities and friendships between those of other lands." (1568-3; April 24, 1938)

"in Egypt during periods when there were the givings to others those things that had become tenets in the activities of those that had followed the building up of what might be termed one of the greater civilizations or periods of approach of man to Maker and ability to manifest same in earth. Little need of physical labor, yet this became a stumbling block—understood little of what was taught by Atlanteans; learned from natives and from Syrians and Chaldeans that had come into land—among those that cleansed themselves through fires of the temple service—aided and counselled emissaries to other lands." (585-2; June 15, 1934)

I call your attention again to the consistency of the Edgar Cayce life readings. Readings given years apart for different individuals may be linked to the same period in history by their corroboration of detail describing this particular period.

When did all of this take place? Each of the following four extracts contain a date:

"In the one before this, we find in that fair country of Alta, or Poseidia proper, in the household of the ruler of that country. This we find nearly ten thousand years before the Prince of Peace came." (288-1; Nov. 20, 1923)

"in the one before this we find in that period when the first understanding of the relation between the All-Creative energy to the putting aside as filial and as penal laws among the people, in the land now known as Egypt, and the time 10,500 years before the Prince of Peace came, as counted by men.

"The entity then in the name of 'Miium' and the entity waited on the priest, and the teacher that gave the lessons or laws, that became rituals of the peoples minds to aid in the understanding of the Creative energy. In the division that arose the entity sided first with the priest, then with the teacher and ruler, and had much to do with the reconciliation that made a united service in that period." (105-2; Jan. 31, 1928)

"In that period when the division arose in the land now known as Egypt. In time as counted 10,500 years before the Prince of Peace came into Egypt in person. The entity among those who were the builders in the physical sense of the homes and places and dwelling places of the people then in power—not as an architect, not as a laborer, rather as the overseer of those than labored, and representing both the native and the alien in their association one with another and the reports of same to the peoples in power." (2483-2; Dec. 15, 1927)

Q.5: "What was the date of the actual beginning and ending of the construction of the Great Pyramid?"
A.5: "Was one hundred years in construction; begun and completed in the period of Araar-aart's time with Hermes and Ra."

142

Q.6: *"What was the date B.C. of that period?"*
A.6: *"10,490 to 10,390 before the Prince of Peace entered Egypt."* (5748-6)

There are a number of life readings that mention records of Atlantean civilization. These records, according to the readings, were carried from Atlantis to Egypt, and an undiscovered pyramid still houses them. There are indications that these records may be discovered in the not too distant future. And such a discovery would rank as one of the greatest in history. The legend of Atlantis would have to be reclassified as fact.

Let us look at the numerous references to these records and their locations. The readings mentioning them seem to refer to the period just discussed, some 10,000 years B.C. This was also about the time the priest Ra-Ta (Edgar Cayce) was recalled from banishment. It was about then that the final destruction of Atlantis occurred and many Atlanteans came into Egypt.

"in Atlantean land in household of the king before the destruction, assisted Alta the scribe in preparing a history of the land. Also at this time there was contention between those of one faith and those of idol worship." (339-1; May 27, 1933)

"in Atlantean land before the final destruction—when the priest came from Egypt to Poseidia to gain understanding of Law of One (or God) that there might be records carried back to Egypt, the entity returned with the priest. Became embroiled in Egyptian politics (pitting of young king against royal native Aarat). Entity made Egypt his home. Rebellions continued in Atlantis, many Atlanteans made exodus to Egypt. Entity aided the Egyptians in chemistry, building, economics, commerce, labor, etc; arts in the broader sense, music, workers in metals and precious stones. Entity had charge of records brought from Atlantis to Egypt." (378-13; 14, 1933)

143

"in Atlantean land of Poseidian peoples when there was the breaking up of the land, among those who came first to Pyrenees and then to Egypt, active in preserving records—using powers called in the present natural sources or electrical forces for propelling vehicles, ships, and for conveniences and communications." (1998-1; Sept. 12, 1939)

"in Poseidia before final breaking up—controlled activities regarding communications with many lands— the flying boats that moved through the air or water were means whereby entity carried many to Iberian land, later to Egypt when it was determined [that the] *records* [were] *to be kept there—found land in turmoil—later with return of priest finally joined with movements for preparation of people for the regeneration of the bodies of 'things' in that period. Again active in communications."* (3184-1; Aug. 28, 1943)

Note that readings given as much as ten years apart mention records of Atlanteans preserved in Egypt. These records are referred to in numerous other individual life readings given months and years apart. Edgar Cayce intimated that they may one day be uncovered.

"in Egypt at time of coalition of natives, king, priest, Atlanteans, etc. Entity among natives in authority as counselor to various groups and historian of that to be preserved, native and Atlantean." (2922-1; Feb. 8, 1943)

"among Atlanteans who came into Egypt for preserving records and promises of Atlantean development—with recall of priest rose to power when there was the union of service and activity toward worship of one God." (2167-1; April 13, 1940)

"before that the entity was in the Egyptian land, among the Atlanteans who came in with those peoples in authority. For, there the entity was one who PERSONALLY cared for the records that were brought by the

144

leaders of that people for preservation in that portion of man's experience in the earth." (2523-1; July 1, 1941)

For one living in the 10,500 B.C. period—*"activities of entity's sojourn then still preserved in the Hall of Records there."* (1182-1; June 1, 1936)

"in Egypt—designed many edifices especially those in which Atlanteans preserved their records—also record house of priests." (3605-1; Jan. 21, 1944)

"entity in the Atlantean and Egyptian land—among those who came into the Egyptian experience for preserving the records of those activities—became a supervisor of the excavations—in studying the old records and in preparing and building the house of records for the Atlanteans as well as a part of the house initiate—or Great Pyramid." (2462-2; June 19, 1941)

"entity aided the priest in the preparation of the manner of building the temple of records that lies just beyond that enigma that still is the mystery of mysteries to those who seek to know what were the manners of thought of the ancient sons who made man, beast—as a part of the consciousness." (2402-2; Nov. 16, 1940)

The last extract suggests that this pyramid or house of records was located in the vicinity of the Sphinx. Another reading confirms this, and says further that similar records exist, or existed, in other parts of the world. It also contains a prophecy about land rising in the Atlantic Ocean.

"Before that we find the entity was in the Atlantean land, when there were the constructive activities of the children of the Law of One, during the periods when the land was being broken up.

"We find the entity was the leading influence for the considering of ways and means in which there would be the preserving of records from the destruction of the lands.

145

"It would be well if this entity were to seek either of the three phases of the ways and means in which those records of the activities of individuals were preserved— the one in the Atlantean land, that sank, which will rise and is rising again; another in the place of the records that leadeth from the Sphinx to the hall of records, in the Egyptian land; and another in the Aryan or Yucatan land, where the temple there is overshadowing same." (2012-1; Sept. 25, 1939)

There are other references indicating that these records may be discovered soon.

"Before that the entity was in the Atlantean land, when there were those periods necessitating the exodus because of the destructive forces being used by the children of Belial.
"The entity was a priestess in the Law of One, and among those who came into the Egyptian land, as the elders in those groups for preserving the records, as well as for preserving a portion of that race, that peoples.
"With the periods of the reconstruction after the return of the priest, the entity joined with those who were active in putting the records in forms that were partially of the old characters of the ancient or early Egyptian, and part in the newer form of the Atlanteans.
"These may be found, especially when the house or tomb of records is opened, in a few years from now." (2537-1; July 17, 1941)

Three more readings mention the possible or even probable discovery of these records.

"in Egypt during the building of many tombs that are being found today [the entity] aided in the construction of the Hall of Records yet to be uncovered." (519-1; Feb. 20, 1934)
"in the Atlantean land when there was the knowledge,

through the teachers and leaders of the Law of One, of the coming destruction of the Atlantean or Poseidian land; the entity journeyed from Atlantis or Poseidia first to the Pyrenees or Portugal land—later to the Egyptian land—during those periods after the recall of Ra-Ta, the priest, when there were attempts for the correlation of knowledge, [the entity] was among the first to set the records that are yet to be discovered or yet to be had of those activities in the Atlantean land, and for the preservation of data that is yet to be found from the chambers of the way between the Sphinx and the pyramid of records." (1486-1; Nov. 26, 1937)

"in Egypt, of the Atlanteans who set about to preserve records— [the entity] came with those groups who were to establish the hall of records or house of records and may directly or indirectly be among those who will yet bring these to light." (3575-2; Jan. 20, 1944)

Another reading offers more definite data on the location of these records and the type of information recorded. Also it again prophesies the rising of land in the Atlantic, land that was once Atlantis.

"The entity Hept-supht led in keeping of the records and buildings that were put in their respective places at this time. This was in the period, as given, of 10,500 years before the entering of the Prince of Peace in the land, to study to become an initiate in or through those same activities that were set up by Hept-supht in this dedication ceremony."

Q.2: "Give in detail what the sealed room contains."

A.2: "A record of Atlantis from the beginning of those periods when the Spirit took form, or began the encasements in that land; and the developments of the peoples throughout their sojourn; together with the record of the first destruction, and the changes that took place in the land; with the record of the sojournings of the peoples and their varied activities in other lands, and a record of the meetings of all the nations or lands, for the activities in the destruction of Atlantis; and the building of the pyramid of initiation, together with whom, what and where the opening of the records would come, that are as copies from the sunken Atlantis. For with the change, it [Atlantis] must rise again.

"In position, this lies—as the sun rises from the waters—as the line of the shadows (or light) falls between the paws of the Sphinx; that was set later as the sentinel or guard and which may not be entered from the connecting chambers from the Sphinx's right paw until the time has been fulfilled when the changes must be active in this sphere of man's experience. Then [it lies] between the Sphinx and the river." (378-16; Oct. 29, 1933)

Although the Nile river is now a good distance from the Sphinx, at the time the pyramid of records was built, it may have been much closer, as indicated by some ancient maps.

In addition to this tomb of records with its history of Atlantean civilization, there are readings indicating that records of *individuals* mentioned in life readings may be found in Egypt.

"Before that we find the entity was in that land now known as the Egyptian, and among the Abyssinian people that were especially influenced by those of the Atlantean land.

"The entity joined rather with those that had come from the Atlantean land, making of self then a priestess and there still may be seen in some of the mountain fastnesses of that land—particularly in the upper Nile where there were those activities in the mountain—the images of the entity may be found near the entrance to the tombs there.

"Then the name was Ai-Ellaiin, and the hieroglyphics will be found like this—The Ibex (the bird of same), the hornheaded man, the Ibex turned in the opposite

148

*direction, the sacred bull of Ipis, the hooded man as of
the Ethiopian people, the cross, the serpent (upright),
the staff with the symbol (that should be the symbol of
the entity throughout its experience) as the B's turned
towards each other or one upright with two loops on
either side of same, with the serpent head two ways from
the top of same."* (559-7; May 25, 1934)

It would be interesting to search the area mentioned in
this reading to see if symbols of the kind described could be
found.

The following extract tells about a particular individual's life during the period under consideration and ends
on a note of prophecy.

*"Before this the entity was in the Egyptian land when
there were those turmoils and trials, when there was the
returning of the priest. The entity was acquainted and
associated with the priest as well as those banished with
the priest, also with those in authority from the
Atlantean land. In Atlantis the entity learned the most,
but in Egypt was the greater period of activity—in the
compiling of data; and portions of that as may yet be
uncovered in the pyramids will be found to have been
put there by the entity, It-Ao."* (2823-1; Sept. 26, 1942)

Besides the records in Egypt there are references to a
contemporary civilization in the Mongoloid or Gobi land.
For those who want to go treasure hunting, here is a clue.

*"We find the entity there made use of the metal known
as iron, or the combinations of iron and copper which
have long since been removed from use in the present; or
copper so tempered by the use of same with a little of the
iron, or in its formation in such a way and manner as to
be hardened by the abilities for same to be used much in
the way that many of those combinations have been
found in the Egyptian, in the Peruvian and portions of*

149

the Chaldean lands and MORE will be found in the Indo-China city yet to be uncovered." (470-22)

"in what is called the Gobi land—entity was priestess in the Temple of Gold that is yet to be unearthed." (2402-2)

"in the land called the Mongoloid or Gobi—among those princesses of that land and there may yet be uncovered in the temple of gold an image of the entity wrought in pure gold in the temple of same." (1167-2)

Let us see what we have learned from piecing together information from a number of individual life readings dealing with incarnations during the period of Egyptian pre-history from 12,000 to 13,000 years ago. A leader Arart from the Caucasian region came into Egypt with his people prior to 10,500 B.C. and conquered it. The Great Pyramid of Giza and the Sphinx were built during the rule of his son Araar-aart. With these invaders came a priest Ra-Ta who attempted to organize religious practices. At about the same time Egypt was being flooded by refugees from sinking Atlantis.

The priest, having become involved in political machinations and consequently a native rebellion, was banished for several years to what later became Abyssinia. However, he was recalled to aid in correlating the activities of the rulers in power, the native Egyptians and the incoming Atlanteans. Under the influence of the priest Ra-Ta, and with the help of the Atlanteans, there began a period of material and spiritual development in Egypt and efforts were made to spread this enlightened culture over the known world. Records—yet to be discovered—of the Atlanteans and their civilization were preserved in Egypt.

Is there any evidence at all to back up Edgar Cayce's statements about a pre-dynastic Egyptian civilization? Does anyone really *know* when the Sphinx and the Great Pyramid were built? Has anyone done any research or conducted any investigations that would establish what Edgar Cayce said about this period as having a factual basis, or conversely, disprove it altogether? Yes, some research has been done. It was done by a young woman, at her own expense, and therefore was financially limited. However, a preliminary report is available on file at A.R.E. headquarters in Virginia Beach. She studied many Edgar Cayce life readings, as well as Egyptian history, and finally went to Egypt to talk to archeologists and look in museums. In this report she compares her findings with data in the Edgar Cayce life readings. It certainly accents the need for further investigation. Miss Blank* found that *The Pyramid Texts* by Samuel B. Mercer (vol. IV, p. 27) refers to the possible northeastern origin of Re and his followers, perhaps from the Caucasus, and to the characteristics of these leader gods, an intellectually and culturally advanced people, who settled in the apex of the delta.

On October 20, 1934, the *Literary Digest* (vol. 118.18) contained a report by Petrie concerning evidence he found of repeated invasions into Egypt from the Caucasus area commencing near the beginning of Egypt's history.

A number of life readings have described the physical appearance of some of the people in Egypt at this 10,500 B.C. period. Many are characterized as having blue or gray eyes and fair hair. Most Egyptians are thought of as being dark-skinned, with dark eyes and dark hair. Miss Blank says that in a tomb between the Sphinx and the Pyramid of Giza is a wall painting of a woman with yellow hair. This hair color has puzzled many archeologists. In the Cairo museum is a small wooden statue with painted blue eyes. Several other statues have blue-gray eyes. There are four heads with Caucasian features in this same museum.

A couple of life readings referring to this early Egpytian period mention robes worn by the priests:

"The robes of the priest would be blue-gray with the hooded portion back from the head, while about the

* Name withheld upon request.

*waist would be a cord of gold color with a purple tassel
or one of the tassels showing."* (585-10)

In the Cairo museum Miss Blank found a small wooden
statue and a large limestone statue wearing what is
described as an unusual dress—*a type of robe* rather than
the kilts Egyptians usually wore in the Old Kingdom
period. Miss Blank copied a number of names given in the
life readings. Among these were Ar-Kar, supposedly buried
in a tomb near the Sphinx; Issii, whose name, according to
a life reading, may be found on many of the inner shrines;
Hermes, who according to the readings was the architect of
the Great Pyramid.

She discovered in *Bibliography III: Memphis,* by Porter
and Moss, that tomb 7101 in the East Cemetery between
the Great Pyramid and the Sphinx is that of Kar.
According to Mrs. Meguid, an English Egyptologist now at
Abydos, the name of Issii can be found inscribed on many
of the inner shrines. In Howard Vyse's *Pyramids of Gizeh,*
Vol. II, in the section on Arab historian, Al Makir's
version, (672 A.D.) is the statement "Hermes built the
Pyamids." Other writers also credit Hermes as being the
architect of the Great Pyramid.

Ibn Batuta—"Hermes the architect of the Great Pyramid to preserve sciences during the flood. . . ."

Watwati—"Hermes built the pyramid. . . ."

Makrimi—"Hermes and his wife reigned in the two
pyramids. . . ." Cites Sorar: "pyramids built by Hermes."
Isis (vol. 30, 1939 pp. 17-37), "The Treaties on the
Egyptian Pyramids" by S. al-Suyuti quotes from Al-
Dimishgi: "some say Hermes built the pyramids."

Miss Blank notes that two life readings refer to early
Egyptian writing:

*"In those periods the entity persuaded many to attempt
activities that would preserve to the peoples what would
be in the present termed recipes, or placards and*

152

drawings and the like that were the first intents brought to the Egyptian peoples (to be sure, NOT to the Atlanteans but to the natives and those who had joined there to preserve such records) and the first attempt to make for a written language." (516-2; Feb. 24, 1934)

The following, which has been quoted before, is repeated because of the reference to the character of early Egyptian writing.

"With the periods of reconstruction after the return of the priest the entity joined with those who were active in putting the records in forms that were partially of the old characters of the ancient or early Egyptians and part in the newer form of the Atlanteans. These may be found, especially when the house or tomb of records is opened, in a few years from now." (2537-1; July 17, 1941)

The American Journal of Archaeology (1952) states that "in the large stone mastaba of Bersen is a subsidiary tomb with unusual hieroglyphics and rare word forms carved on the doors."

Vyse's *Pyramids of Gizeh,* Vol. I contains this statement: "in the upper relieving chamber above the King's chamber in the Great Pyramid are hieroglyphic marks difficult to decipher."

Readings previously quoted indicate that the Sphinx was built a very long time ago—probably over 10,000 years B.C. References are also made to a record chamber, not yet discovered, near the Sphinx.

Miss Blank records the following from *Excavations at Giza, Sphinx,* Vol. VIII by Dr. Selim Hassan. Page 113 concerns an Inventory Stela:

"This stela claims the temple of Isis (near the Great Pyramid) was found by Khufu and rebuilt by him and also refers to repairs made on the Sphinx due to damage by lightning. If true this would date both the temple and the Sphinx before Khufu (IV Dynasty, 2900 B.C.) This stela is dedicated to 'Isis, Mistress of the Pyramids' which is inexplicable by present theories as Khufu is considered the first King to have built a pyramid in this area. Some consider this Inventory Stela a copy or forgery. However, the repair measurements given with regard to the Sphinx correspond with scar measurements still visible. Also references to the location of the House of Osiris in relation to the House of Isis and the Sphinx were accurate and the House of Osiris was found as described."

Miss Blank examined the Sphinx and found that the inner contours of the two forepaws have been filled in with large limestone block, which are visible where the outer double casing of brickwork is incomplete. The right hindpaw can also be seen to be completely composed of similar large limestone blocks. According to Mrs. Meguid, who was working with Dr. Hassan when he cleared the sand from the site, there were large limestone blocks in the rear of the body where the tail begins. These were not examined, but covered with brickwork, nor were the other blocks examined.

Due east of the Sphinx, on the other side of the road leading to the Great Pyramid, is a small sand hill. Abde Salam investigated it but did not continue far enough west. He found some blackened limestone that seemed to be part of an Old Kingdom façade which he thought might have come from a small temple. Since there was supposed to have been a small pyramid over the spot where the record chamber was, this may or may not be indicative.

Miss Blank concludes her report:

"The evidence, though slight and not conclusive, is promising. The visual evidence alone is sufficient as a basis for a more thorough examination because there is no known record of such. Dr. Selim Hassan cleared the sand from the Sphinx and repaired damaged parts but he removed no stones. There is almost no contemporary information on the Sphinx. Who built it and why is still mainly conjecture. Foundation deposits containing such information were usually placed under most temples; so,

154

possibly some such might be found under one of the large limestone blocks composing the paws. There is no complete study of the Sphinx available. Such a reference work is needed and would constitute a valuable contribution to Egyptology."

Miss Blank, since her first trip to Egypt, has returned to California for additional courses in early Egyptian history. She subsequently returned to Egypt for further archeological explorations, but her work was interrupted by the Middle East crisis.

CHAPTER 6

The Shadow of Atlantis

Many people find it difficult to accept the possibility that the advanced civilization of Atlantis, described by Edgar Cayce, could have existed and then disappeared with so little trace. However, a little reflection shows that this is not as impossible as it first seems. Less than a hundred years ago only science fiction writers could conceive of such things as television, atomic submarines and the hydrogen bomb, wonder drugs and regular jet flights to Europe. In the last fifty years many nations have disappeared in the chaos of two world wars; many new ones have arisen. If one considers the dependence of our present civilization on transportation and electric power it is easy to see that an atomic war, while it might not end civilization entirely, could literally blast mankind back to the stone age. Records exist of mighty civilizations of the past that have risen and fallen as a result of much less catastrophic events than those that befell Atlantis. It is probable that in another five thousand years even their names will be forgotten.

Thus, it is not so strange that a country whose very land area lies at the bottom of the Atlantic Ocean and whose last inhabitants mixed with other nations over twelve thousand years ago should leave little trace. What is truly remarkable is that even a legend remains to mark the demise of what must have been an extraordinary nation, one similar in many ways to our own.

It is this similarity that is stressed in the Edgar Cayce life readings—for the same people are reincarnating again at this time. The urges, talents and abilities of Atlanteans are manifested in individuals today. To return to the two individuals, past Atlanteans, mentioned at the beginning of this book, the same sort of thing is happening on a grand scale in our world today. In the last fifty years there has been more scientific advancement than in all recorded history. Why this sudden spurt? The "death rays" and "terrible crystals" described in the Edgar Cayce life readings sound as much like modern lasers and atomic power plants as it would have been possible to describe in the early 20's and 30's when many of these readings were given. The slaves, "automatons" or "things" described in the Atlantean life readings seem to have returned to haunt the world in the underprivileged, uneducated, uncared-for masses of humanity. Here in America, where scientific development has reached its greatest peaks, the race problem has come into sharpest focus. In Atlantis man faced a choice between following the "Sons of the Law of One" (meaning his realization of his relationship to God) and the Sons of Belial (meaning the use of his creative powers for self-aggrandizement). Then the strife among men brought physical destruction in the earth. Now man is again being forced to choose between selfishness and unselfishness. Man now has in his hands the capacity for a better life for himself. He can use his scientific knowledge to improve the lot of all. He also has in his hands the means to bring about world destruction rivaling that of Atlantis.

There are some indications in the readings that future destruction and changes may come from natural causes. One was given in 1940 and the other in 1943.

"Poseidia will be among the first portions of Atlantis to rise again—expect it '68 and '69—not so far away." (958-3; June 28, 1940)

". . . in Atlantis in the period of the first upheavals and destruction that came to the land, as must in the next

157

generation to come to other land." (3209-2; Dec. 30, 1943)

Funk and Wagnalls' dictionary gives a definition of a generation as, "a step or degree in natural descent; the period between successive steps in natural descent, usually taken as 30 years in humans."

Webster's dictionary gives a similar definition: "the ordinary period of time at which one rank follows another, or father is succeeded by child—usually taken to be about 33 years."

Reading 3209-2 was given in 1943, suggesting that by 1976 there will be upheavals and destruction in some existing land areas. Presumably this will have had at least its beginning in 1968-69. These upheavals and changes may refer to volcanic or earthquake activity that will result in the appearance of land in the Atlantic, land that may have been a portion of Atlantis. Archeological explorations of this land would then be possible.

Here are things one can watch for. Perhaps the next generation will see the question of Atlantis answered conclusively. Unfortunately some rather drastic earth changes are predicted during the next thirty to forty years, some probably beginning in the near future.

"As to the changes physical again: The earth will be broken up in the western portion of America. The greater portion of Japan must go into the sea. The upper portion of Europe will be changed as in the twinkling of an eye. Land will appear off the east coast of America.

"There will be upheavals in the Arctic and in the Antarctic that will make for the eruption of volcanoes in the Torrid areas, and there will be the shifting then of the poles—so that where there have been those of a frigid or semitropical will become the more tropical, and moss and fern will grow.

"And these will begin in those periods in '58 to '98 when these will be proclaimed as the periods when His Light

will be seen again in the clouds." (3976-15; January 19, 1934)

Q.12: *"How soon will the changes in the earth's activity begin to be apparent?"*

A.12: *"When there is the first breaking-up of some conditions in the South Sea (that's South Pacific, to be sure), and those as apparent in the sinking or arising of that which is almost opposite to it, or in the Mediterranean, and the Aetna (Etna?) area. Then we may know it has begun."*

Q.14: *"Will there be any physical changes in the earth's surface in North America? If so, what sections will be affected, and how?"*

A.14: *"All over the country we will find many physical changes of a minor or greater degree. The greater change, as we will find, in America, will be the North Atlantic Seaboard. Watch New York!"* (311-8; MS-7; April 9, 1932)

"As to conditions in the geography of the world, of the country, changes here are gradually coming about. Many portions of the east coast will be disturbed, as well as many portions of the west coast, as well as the central portion of the United States.

"In the next few years, lands will appear in the Atlantic as well as in the Pacific. And what is the coast line now of many a land will be bed of the ocean. Even many of the battlefields of the present [1941] will be ocean, will be the seas, the bays, the lands over which the new order will carry on their trade as one with another.

"Portions of the now east coast of New York, or New York City itself, will in the main disappear. This will be another generation, though, here; while the southern portions of Carolina, Georgia, these will disappear. This will be much sooner.

"The waters of the lakes [Great Lakes] will empty into the Gulf [Gulf of Mexico], rather than the waterway over which such discussions have been recently made. . . . [St. Lawrence Seaway].

159

"Then the area where the entity (1152) is now located [Virginia Beach] will be among the safety lands—as will be portions of what is now Ohio, Indiana and Illinois and much of the southern portion of Canada, and the eastern portion of Canada; while the western land, much of that is to be disturbed in this land, as, of course, much in other lands." (1152-11; MS-3; Aug. 13, 1941)

"The earth will be broken up in many places. The early portion will see a change in the physical aspect of the west coast of America. There will be open waters in the northern portion of Greenland. There will be new lands seen off the Carribean Sea and dry land will appear— South America shall be shaken from the uppermost portion to the end, and in the Antarctic off Tierra Del Fuego, land, and a strait with rushing waters." (3976- 15; Jan. 19, 1934)

These statements are all about future events. They certainly offer a means for future generations to check the accuracy of this portion of the Edgar Cayce readings. In fact, many people living today may witness some of these events.

How do these predictions relate to Atlantis? Many people today were Atlanteans, who lived to see their country being broken up physically. Many of these same people may go through a similar experience in the years ahead.

In considering what has been said about Atlantis, it is important to remember that the picture here presented does not come from what Edgar Cayce said in merely one or two readings. The information was gleaned from over 650 life readings which were given over a period of twenty-one years. These life readings were mainly for the benefit of the individuals concerned and dealt also with incarnations other than Atlantean. One might say the information contained in these readings concerning Atlantis is incidental, yet the internal consistency and chronological sequence of this Atlantean information is amazing. These points, together with the fact that the accuracy of Edgar Cayce's physical diagnoses (the physical readings) has been verified beyond question, are thought-provoking, to say the least.

If Edgar Cayce is right, many people are living today who lived in one or more of the eras of Atlantean disturbances. The problems facing individuals and nations now are not very different from those these same individuals and similar nations faced in the past. We all have another choice, another chance to improve our lot. We may make this choice as a nation or as individuals or both.

I believe in free will, and do not think that the future is fixed. There are many people who have been warned of possible future disasters, in dreams for example, and who took heed and avoided the disaster. There is a classic example in the Book of Jonah in the Bible of a whole city repenting and being spared the wrath of God. If man—on a national and individual level—can become aware of his true nature and his relationship to God he may be able to avoid repeating past mistakes.

I have heard Hugh Lynn Cayce, Director of the A.R.E., say that the effect of the philosophy expressed in the Edgar Cayce readings on individuals is the most valuable part of the work of the Association for Research and Enlightenment. Each person must decide for himself whether or not contact with this work has changed his life in any way, or made him a better individual by expanding his consciousness.

Edgar Cayce's work brought him fame, but not fortune. He was never wealthy, or even well-to-do. I remember thinking many times that if I could just have some of life's luxuries, I might get along without the necessities. This worried Edgar Cayce and his family sometimes. He was human, and in the process of helping others, it seemed natural that he should ask why he couldn't help himself materially. In fact, he once turned to the readings with this very question:

161

"In consideration of the fact that Edgar Cayce is devoting his entire time to work, give the reason for his not being able to obtain sufficient financial support for him and his family's material sustenance, and how may he, Edgar Cayce, correct this condition?"

A.8: *"Live closer to Him Who giveth all good and perfect gifts, and ask and ye shall receive; knock and it shall be opened unto you. Give and it shall be returned fourfold. Give, give, give, if you would receive. There has never been the lack of necessities, neither will there be, so long as adhering to the Lord's Way is kept first and foremost."* (254-11)

A quotation from another reading, 262-89, says:

"most of us think we need a great deal more than we do."

These same problems perplex us today. To quote *The Virginian Pilot* of June 21, 1963: "Do we need every thing we want? Probably not. And probably the wishing and worrying we expend yearning for things we want but don't really need detracts considerably from our sense of wellbeing.

"Nearly all Americans can meet basic needs. Even those on minimum pensions in retirement have a roof over their heads, sufficient food and clothing, some sort of medical care, access to a television set and enough left over for an occasional ice cream soda.

"But instead of enjoying these minimum gifts—which would be regarded as maximum blessings by millions in other parts of the world—many choose to enumerate and contemplate the things they lack and make themselves restless and discontented in the process.

"As we grow older and encounter a diminishing income, we must be practical in coping with the circumstances. Before spending our money on things which attract and appeal to us, we should get into the habit of asking whether or not we need it, or whether we merely want it."

We go through life acquiring possessions that we must eventually leave here. How much better it would be to turn our attention to developing spiritual qualities that will abide with us throughout eternity!

Such problems are the concern of thoughtful men. In 1959, Dr. Laurence M. Gould, president of Carleton College in Minnesota, gave an address entitled "Why Men Survive." He pointed out that nineteen out of twenty-one notable civilizations "died from within." Dr. Gould said, "The greatest threat to ours is not atom bombs or guided missiles, but neglect of the spiritual forces that make us wish to be right and noble." He concluded, "If America is to grow great we must stop gagging at the word 'spiritual.' Our task is to rediscover and reassert our faith in the spiritual, nonutilitarian values on which American life has really rested from its beginning."

Dr. Gould echoes some Edgar Cayce readings. I offer the following as an example of these:

"What is your God? Are your ambitions only set in what you shall eat tomorrow, or wherewith you shall be clothed? You of little faith, little hope that allow such to become paramount issues in your own consciousness. Know you not that you are His? For you are of His making! He has not willed that you should perish, but has left it with you as to whether you will ever become aware of your relationship with Him or not!" (281-41)

"Though there may be worlds, many universes, even solar systems greater than our own (the earth is a mere speck when considered even with our own solar system) yet the soul of man, your soul, encompasses all in this solar system or in others. For we are joint heirs with the universal force we call God, if we seek to do His bidding." (5755-2)

This philosophy is not intended as a sermon. Edgar Cayce never wanted to start a new cult or religion.

Association for Research and Enlightenment members do not form a strange sect. The readings repeatedly say that the thought expressed should not pull you away from your church, but should make you a better Methodist, Presbyterian, Catholic, Jew, Mormon, or whatever you are. Edgar Cayce's philosophy is intended to expand your consciousness to broader and more rational concepts of your own faith, to help you discover your relationship to God. And here, I think, lies the greatest appeal of the Edgar Cayce life readings for individuals.

REFERENCES

A. References on Reincarnation

Cayce, Hugh Lynn, *Venture Inward* (New York: Harper & Row, 1964). Available in reprint from Paperback Library, Inc.

Cerminara, Gina, *Many Mansions* (New York: William Sloan Associates, 1950).

——————, *The World Within* (New York: William Sloan Associates, 1957).

Ducasse, C. J., "How the Case for Bridey Murphy Stands Today," *Journal of the American Society for Psychical Research* (1960).

Head, Joseph, and Cranston, *Reincarnation: An East-West Anthology* (New York: The Julian Press, 1961).

Langley, Noel, *Edgar Cayce on Reincarnation* (New York: Paperback Library, Inc., 1967). Available in hardcover from Hawthorn Books, Inc.

Stearn, Jess, *Edgar Cayce—The Sleeping Prophet* (New York: Doubleday, 1967).

Stevenson, Ian, "Twenty Cases Suggestive of Reincarnation," *The American Society for Psychical Research,* XXVI (September, 1966).

Sugrue, Thomas, *There Is A River* (New York: Henry Holt & Co., 1942).

Weatherhead, Leslie D., *The Case for Reincarnation* (Surrey, England: M. C. Peto, 1958).

B. References on Atlantis

Bjorkman, Edwin, *The Search for Atlantis* (New York: Alfred A. Knopf, 1927).

Braghine, Alexander, *The Shadow of Atlantis* (New York: E. P. Dutton, 1940).

Bromwell, James, *Lost Atlantis* (London: Cobden-Sanderson, 1937).

Cayce, Edgar Evans, *Atlantis—Fact or Fiction?* (Virginia Beach, Va.: A.R.E. Press, 1962).

Donnelly, Ignatius, *Atlantis, the Antediluvian World,* revised by Egerton Sykes (New York: Harper & Brothers, 1949).

Ewing, Maurice, "Lost Continent Called Myth," *Science Digest* (April, 1949).

Gardner, Martin, *In the Name of Science* (New York: Putnam, 1952).

Graves, Robert, "What Happened to Atlantis?" *Atlantic Monthly* (October, 1953).

Spence, Lewis, *The History of Atlantis* (New York: David McKay Co., 1927).

C. Miscellaneous

Bennett, W. C., *Ancient Arts of the Andes* (New York: Museum of Modern Art, and Minneapolis Institute of Art and California Palace of the Legion of Honor, 1954).

Coon, C. S., *Origin of the Races* (New York: Alfred A. Knopf, 1962).

Dunbar, C. O., *Historical Geology* (New York: John Wiley and Sons, 1949).

Ferguson, T. S., *One Fold and One Shepherd* (Books of California, 1958).

Kolbe, R. W., "Fresh Water Diatoms from Atlantic Deep-Sea Sediments," *Science,* vol. 126 (1957), 1053-1056.

Malaise, Rene, *Ocean Bottom Investigations and Their Bearings on Geology* (Sweden: Geologiska Foreningens I Stockholm Forhandlingar, March-April 1957).

Mellis, O., "Sedimentation in the Romanche Deep," *International Geological Review,* I, 9 (1958), 50-58.

"Underwater Discoveries in the Straits of Florida," *Military Engineer,* LI, 543 (1959), 403.

Waters, Frank, *Book of the Hopi* (New York: The Viking Press, Inc., 1963).

* * * *

NOTE: A complete list of the Edgar Cayce life readings referring to Atlantis is on file at the Association for Research and Enlightenment at Virginia Beach, Virginia.

THE A. R. E. TODAY

Out of the wealth of material in the Cayce files grew the Edgar Cayce Foundation and its affiliated organizations, The Association for Research and Enlightenment, Inc., and The Edgar Cayce Publishing Co., all headquartered in the same building at Virginia Beach.

The Foundation is engaged in the gigantic task of indexing and cross-indexing the hundreds of subjects discussed in the readings. Because of their age, the papers are rapidly deteriorating, and they are now being microfilmed for safekeeping and ready reference. The subject matter almost blankets the field of human thought: from the value of peanuts to the building of the Great Pyramid; from how to get rid of pinworms to prophecy of the future.

The Association for Research and Enlightenment is an open-membership, nonprofit organization chartered under the laws of the Commonwealth of Virginia to carry on psychic research. It is devoted to the study of the readings and conducts numerous experiments in psychic phenomena. It also cooperates with and encourages investigation by qualified persons in the fields of medicine, psychology and theology. The active membership of the A.R.E., as it is usually called, is made up of people of all religious faiths and many nationalities, including foreign countries. Strangely, they all seem to be able to reconcile their faiths with the metaphysical philosophy emerging from the Cayce readings. They come from all walks of life; there are doctors, lawyers, ministers, artists, businessmen, school teachers, students, working people, housewives.

The Association, governed by a board of trustees, conducts conferences at the Virginia Beach headquarters and regional conferences in New York, Dallas, Denver, Los Angeles and other large cities.

The Cayce Foundation and its affiliated organizations occupy a large, rambling, three-story frame building of shore architecture. Standing on the highest elevation at Virginia Beach, the building and grounds take up a full city block and face the Atlantic Ocean, a block away.

Hundreds of visitors come every year. Besides the library and offices, there are overnight guest rooms, a cafeteria, lobby, publications room and printing press. With the steadily growing membership and interest, a staff of thirty-five workers, mostly volunteers, handles volumes of inquiries, special requests, lecture announcements and literature. Visitors are shown about the plant and grounds with its broad, tiled veranda overlooking the ocean. Everyone wants to see the fireproof vault and the readings.

To the skeptic there is an appropriate answer: in the words of Abraham Lincoln, "No man has a good enough memory to be a successful liar."

EDGAR EVANS CAYCE

The author of EDGAR CAYCE ON ATLANTIS is the youngest son of the famous clairvoyant Edgar Cayce and his wife, Gertrude. Born in Selma, Alabama, in 1919, he moved with the family to Virginia Beach, Virginia, in 1925. After graduating from high school as valedictorian, he attended Duke University and in 1939 received a Bachelor of Science degree in electrical engineering. World War II provided a four and a half year interlude in which he rose from the status of private in the Army to captain in charge of a radar company in the Air Corps.

As a registered professional engineer in the State of Virginia, he is active as a member of the National Society of Professional Engineers and the Institute of Electrical and Electronic Engineers.

Mr. Cayce is married and the father of two children. He is at the present time Chairman of the Board of Trustees of the Association for Research and Enlightenment, the organization which is interested in preserving and studying the transcripts of psychic data left by his late father. The present book, EDGAR CAYCE ON ATLANTIS, is based on the author's meticulous research into those records.

EDGAR CAYCE ON E.S.P.

by Doris Agee

under the editorship of Hugh Lynn Cayce

The definitive work on the celebrated prophet's extraordinary achievements in parapsychological phenomena. ESP topics covered include: out-of-body travel; unusual incidences of clairvoyance; auras; telepathy; missing persons; precognition and prophecy; dreams; psychic development in individuals . . . every aspect of Extrasensory Perception!

☐ (88-196, $1.50)

EDGAR CAYCE ON RELIGION AND PSYCHIC EXPERIENCE

by Harmon Hartzell Bro, Ph.D.

In this illuminating book Dr. Harmon Bro shows, through a detailed analysis of the Cayce readings, that such experiences a
* using hunches for guidance
* reading auras
* communicating with the dead
* remembering past incarnations
can become as natural as breathing to the person growing spiritually.

☐ (88-103, $1.50)

EDGAR CAYCE ON THE DEAD SEA SCROLLS

by Glenn D. Kittler

under the editorship of Hugh Lynn Cayce

Before the discovery of the Dead Sea Scrolls, no acknowledge expert in history or religion ever put forth the possibility tha Jesus, Mary, Joseph, John the Baptist, and other leading fig ures in the Gospels were associated in any way with th Essenes. Yet for twenty years, the Life Readings given b Edgar Cayce had been producing information regarding th association.

☐ (88-147, $1.50)

STRANGER IN THE EARTH

by Thomas Sugrue

Thomas Sugrue takes you on an illuminating journey of self-discovery. Follow him to Virginia Beach, to the home of Edgar Cayce, America's most famous clairvoyant; listen with him as he receives his first life reading. Go with him as he studies the mystery religions; go with him to Palestine, to Egypt; and follow him into his own mind—the heights of its inspiration and the depths of its despair.

☐ (65-456, 95¢)

HIGH PLAY

Turning On Without Drugs
The Edgar Cayce Approach

by Harmon Hartzell Bro, Ph.D.

Psychotherapist Harmon H. Bro, leading interpreter of Edgar Cayce, delves into the varieties of consciousness-altering experiences that can be achieved without drugs. Drawing on his work with Cayce and case histories, Bro explores encounter groups, meditation, LSD therapy and other areas.

☐ (66-738, $1.25)

EDGAR CAYCE ON HEALING
by Mary Ellen Carter and
William A. McGarey, M.D.

Of the more than 14,000 Edgar Cayce readings recorded, nearly 9,000 deal with matters of health. Cayce's ability to diagnose, while in trance, the physical disorders of a person he had never met, who might be hundreds of miles away, and then suggest effective treatment, remains one of the most astonishing psychic feats of all times.

In **Edgar Cayce on Healing**, a dozen of these cases are scrutinized by a professional writer, Mary Ellen Carter, and a modern doctor of medicine, William A. McGarey. What sort of person consulted Edgar Cayce? What did the readings mean to those who received them? What light does the quarter-century of medical advance since Cayce's death shed on his often-unorthodox recommendations for treatment? The often-surprising answers make this book fascinating reading for everyone interested in Edgar Cayce, in psychic phenomena, and in medical science.

☐ (88-171, $1.50)

EDGAR CAYCE ON JESUS
AND HIS CHURCH
by Anne Read

under the editorship of Hugh Lynn Cayce

Using many of Edgar Cayce's own words, Anne Read provides a remarkably full, intimately detailed account of the life, death and resurrection of Jesus.

☐ (88-156, $1.50)